LEE COUNTY LIBRARY
SANFORD, N. C.

THE LAST HILL

By the same Author

BOMB RUN

THE LAST HILL
Spencer Dunmore

William Morrow & Company, Inc.
New York 1973

Copyright © 1973 by Spencer Dunmore

Published in Great Britain under the title
Tower of Strength.

All rights reserved. No part of this book may be reproduced or utilized in any form or by any means, electronic or mechanical, including photocopying, recording or by any information storage and retrieval system, without permission in writing from the Publisher. Inquiries should be addressed to William Morrow and Company, Inc., 105 Madison Ave., New York, N.Y. 10016.

Printed in the United States of America.

Library of Congress Cataloging in Publication Data
Dunmore, Spencer, (date)
   The last hill.

  1. World War, 1939-1945—Fiction. I. Title.
PZ4.D922Las3 [PR6054.U53]   813'.5'4   73-664
ISBN 0-688-00167-X

For Eric Dunmore, who was there.
And for Jean, of course.

THE LAST HILL

1

It was raining hard when the aircraft landed at Kuala Lumpur. At my shoulder the raindrops danced across the window in two orderly lines. Very neat and military. I shivered, but not because of the temperature. Before we had turned off the runway the sun was shining again. Now the raindrops sparkled like Woolworth jewellery. The aircraft trundled to the terminal and stopped. I waited until all the other passengers were shuffling to the exit before I moved. I was in no hurry. Besides, I was nervous. I had spent the flight from Singapore looking at the ground and feeling slightly sick and wishing I had stayed at home in Hampstead. And I remember continually telling myself to snap out of it—which was utterly pointless, because I was quite incapable of doing anything of the sort.

In the terminal Mr Appleby was waiting, as arranged. He welcomed me to Malaya. 'Have you been here before, Mr Cornish?'

'Once,' I told him.

As we clambered into his Mini, the rain started again.

'Can we still go?' I asked.

'Rather. Just a shower. Piece of cake.'

I tried to look pleased.

We drove away from the terminal area, past the main hangars and administrative buildings, and turned in behind a low structure, outside which stood four small aeroplanes.

'Here we are, Mr Cornish.' Appleby leant across and opened the car door. He was a pleasant man, about fifty, ex-Air Force. ('Flew Mossies from the Arakan, old man,' he told me later. 'But I couldn't stick it in the Old Country afterwards. Austerity era. Came back East. Wife hated it. Buzzed off home to Mother. Ah well.')

I followed him through a bright red door into a minute office containing two desks, three chairs, a telephone, a jug of dusty water and an aero-navigational chart on one wall.

I studied the chart but the place wasn't marked. I hadn't expected it to be. 'If I remember correctly, it's about here,' I told Appleby. 'On that road. It's a fairly important highway. Or was.'

Appleby clicked his tongue cheerfully as he jabbed a forefinger at the chart. 'Then the nearest field is here, at Segakab. Fifteen miles, twenty at the most, from where you want to go. I should think there'll be someone who can drive you from there.'

I asked him if it might be possible to confirm that fact before we set off. He grinned in his friendly way and said rather, no reason at all why not; he would ring up there and then—*if* he could get through, which wasn't at all a sure thing at the best of times, but no harm in trying, what? Operators of charter-flight firms appear to be cast in the same mould the world over: engaging chaps but rather too casual for comfort.

While Appleby was telephoning I stood at the window and pretended to watch the airport goings-on. What I was really doing was asking myself whether it wouldn't be sensible to pay Mr Appleby *now* for his time, trouble and telephone call, then catch the next plane home, to family and agency and clients and the world I belonged to. Of course it would.

The trouble was, I wanted to see that place again. I wanted to walk on that ground again. And I think I also had a hope, a faint hope, that going there might convince me there had been some meaning in what happened. But I rather doubted it.

Appleby hung up the telephone with a triumphant flourish. 'A chap is going to meet us at the field. He says he has a good car. He's probably lying but with a bit of luck he'll get you where you want to go.'

We went outside and boarded one of the aircraft. It was fiendishly hot and sour-smelling in the diminutive cabin.

'Sorry, old man. Kept the door closed because of the rain. Never mind, soon be nice and cool when we get airborne.' After starting the engine and rapping on dials, he took a hand-mike from a hook beneath the instrument panel and asked the tower for permission to taxi. He was leaving, he told the tower, on a trip to Segakab.

With a mental case for a passenger, I thought.

We took off, wobbling into the air like a paper boat on turbulent waters. A wing dropped; the ground tilted alarmingly. Smiling, Appleby turned the wheel with a casual left hand; smoothly and unhurriedly his legs moved as he worked the rudder pedals.

'Wee bit bumpy,' he observed.

I said I had noticed.

'All right, old man?'

I nodded.

'Good show.'

With another bump the little machine climbed into calmer air. Below us the jungle stretched like an ocean of green in every conceivable shade. I loosened my tie. From the air the *ulu* appears innocent enough; it has a lush, luxurious look about it. But try hacking your way through it with a *machete* or a Malayan *parang*. It will mock your puny efforts; it will blunt your weapons on tree-trunks that are iron-hard; it will sap your energy in soaking, blinding heat.

3

It will allow you to see no more than a few yards. It will do its very best to kill you.

I hated and feared the jungle from the first day I saw it. Such an orgy of fertility: too much life: vines, shoots, trees, flowers of God-knows-how-many varieties and colours, all fighting with lunatic enthusiasm for the specks of sunlight that manage to flicker through from above—fighting solely to drink in sufficient energy to continue fighting.

We climbed higher and higher until the temperature in the cabin became almost bearable.

'Nasty spot for engine trouble,' said Appleby with his perpetual grin. 'I always like lots of height when I'm over the allotment. That's what I call it—the allotment.'

I asked him if he had ever had engine trouble over the allotment. He shook his head, seeming to suggest that he had had plenty of opportunities but had rejected them all.

'Smoke if you want to, old man.'

I declined. I had given up smoking a few months after those first warnings. I wasn't going to risk my precious being for the sake of a couple of packets a day. The shedding of the tobacco habit put some pounds on me. I had to have all my clothes altered. But I was told that the extra weight suited me, that I was too thin before. It is one of the pleasanter aspects of being a chairman of the board that one is told such things.

The ground rolled and dipped as hill succeeded valley. The mountains were partially hidden in mist. At the airport, an Immigration man had asked me whether I had come on business or pleasure. I told him pleasure but I suppose it would have been more accurate to say that my trip was for medical reasons: treatment of a polyp on the memory.

Appleby asked how things were in the Old Country.

He had been planning a visit for years but his flying school and charter business kept him too busy. 'I'd like to see London again,' he said. 'Always liked London. Used to go there on leaves. Has it changed much? Yes, I suppose it has. Everything changes. It's one of the things you realize as you get older, isn't it? No use hanging on to the old things, the old values. They'll soon be gone, replaced by something else. May be better, may be worse. Can't be sure. But it'll be different.'

Trust me to pick a philosophical pilot. I looked down at the right main wheel as it traced a path across the jungle. How many Englishmen died on that spot? And that spot? And how many Japanese? What a stupid waste of time and effort and lives the whole thing had turned out to be. All that happened was that the British were defeated and eventually cleared out. And no doubt we would have cleared out even if the Japanese hadn't pushed us.

I had told Eleanor I was going on a business trip. It was easier than telling her the truth. Infinitely so. After all, how could I expect to convey to her just why I wanted-and-yet-didn't-want to go back to the damned place, when I really didn't know myself?

A river wound a tortuous path through the vegetation, shimmering in the sun as if made of metal. Soon it vanished from view, concealed by the tall trees on either bank.

Appleby had a map folded into an oblong of paper that represented the territory over which we were flying. He kept peering at the map then glancing over the side of the aircraft, frowning. I hoped he knew where we were. Almost at once, as if in reply to my doubts, he grinned and angled a wing at the jungle.

'There's your road, old man!' He jabbed a finger at a slender ribbon of black far below.

I nodded soberly. But my heart did a sort of double-

5

shuffle.

'Can't be too far now.' Appleby eased back the throttle; the engine softened its roar. 'We'll go down and have a closer look-see.' The altimeter began to unwind.

That bloody road. Was it paved now, or was it still a nightmare of pot-holes and stones and mud? Once upon a beastly time I had trudged every yard of it. Stupid with fatigue and frightened of snipers and snakes and anything else that moved. Particularly anything Japanese. For hour after funky hour I had trudged on, always peering up at the trees that loomed over us like malevolent witches. The Japanese snipers were deadly—and fond of officers as targets. One nearly hit me. But he got a lance-corporal instead. How lucky I was, I thought at the time. Then I wondered; the lance-jack went back to ride in an Austin van, nursing a minor flesh wound. The Austin was Wounded Transport. It constituted one-third of our motor fleet. The other two trucks, 3-ton Bedfords, carried some of our food and ammunition. A procession of sad-eyed mules carried the rest. We were proceeding to a hill in Sector 14F where, it was said, we would take up positions and form part of the line of Imperial Troops who, it was said, would stop the Japanese in their southwards tracks. We plodded on. Our spirits were low because we had been retreating for more than a month, all the way down the peninsula, outflanked and outfought at every turn. We hated the Japanese because they were so terrifyingly efficient; we hated our generals for precisely the opposite reason. A month before we had been a rifle battalion, an orderly, organized component of a regiment of the British Army. But a couple of hundred men had vanished along the way; a company of Highlanders had joined us, followed by other bewildered fragments of a disintegrating army. Communications were a shambles, a bloody disgrace; no one knew where anyone was, friend or foe. All we knew was that we had to press on.

'That must be your place ahead,' said Appleby, pointing.

Your place. I swallowed. Not my place; for God's sake don't call it that.

My shirt was becoming glued to my back again as we neared the ground. Ah, there it was! How insignificant it looked. A mere pimple in the jungle, surrounded by larger hills. The road still travelled straight up the northern face of the hill, then turned at right angles; it hadn't changed. The village—*kampong* to the Malays—straddled the road near the turn. A cosy, tidy-looking place. I was glad to see that it had been built again. We and the Japanese had done our zealous best to wipe it off the face of the earth. And we had very nearly succeeded.

Appleby banked steeply.

'That it?'

I nodded as the hill turned beneath me. The north face, the east, the south, the west ... I looked down at it as I might have looked at a model. What was spread before me was an excellent facsimile, but it wouldn't be the real thing until I stood on it again.

A man in a white shirt and dark shorts came walking out of the trees. He stopped and looked up, shielding his eyes with one hand. No doubt he was wondering why the little aeroplane was circling his village.

I suddenly realized something. The pilot of the Zero must have seen the place almost exactly as I was seeing it. Except that now there was no tattered thread of troops winding up the hill—and no terrified infantry captain named David Cornish running for his life.

2

Cornish saw the Zero at the same moment he heard it. From behind the hill it came, insanely low, spitting little dots of fire from its nose and wings, a blurring vision of glinting cylinders and olive paint with great red blobs on its metallic flank.

'Oh, golly,' said someone inadequately.

Cornish discovered he was on one knee at the side of the road, revolver in hand. He didn't remember taking the thing out of its holster. He put it back. His hand shook. Around him, rifle bolts slammed home in a clattering burst of sound, mechanical but tinny and insubstantial; rifles were no match for the hurtling monster.

'Take cover!' Cornish yelled at the crouched men with the rifles angling at the sky.

But the Zero was already out of sight. Above, a tree trembled as if in relief.

'Everyone all right?'

His tongue slithered over suddenly-dry lips as he quickly scanned the immediate area. The men were moving, thank God. No lifeless lumps splashing blood all over the place. The men were all taut necks and scruffy chins as they searched the sky. There hadn't been time to shave that morning.

'We're OK, sir,' reported Corporal Hall, darting across the road, bent almost double. 'No one hit.'

'Good. Thank you, Corporal.'

Cornish wondered whether there were any more Jap

planes about. It seemed likely. He felt exposed. Here on the hill there was nowhere to hide. Foul as the jungle was, it did at least provide plenty of cover.

'Look out!'

'Mind your 'ead!'

The Zero again. Pretty. It streaked in over the trees like the next act at the Hendon Air Display.

Christ ... He felt his fingernails digging deeply into his palms; but still he clenched his fists to stop them shaking...

Rifles and machine-guns—the Brens on the lorries—crackled in fury. Cornish saw the Jap's fire hitting the road, sending up small eruptions of stones. A man fell—apparently hit—then scrambled to his feet and ran for cover.

'I think we got the bugger,' said Corporal Hall.

'What?'

'Look, sir.' The corporal pointed. 'We hit him.'

God yes. Someone had hit. Smoke was gushing out of the engine. As if in pain, the Zero twisted and faltered. It flew out over the jungle, then turned.

'He's coming back!'

'The daft sod,' said someone in outraged tones.

'Down! Get down!' Cornish yelled. But no, it wasn't a yell. As he hurled himself full length, he knew it had been a screech, a cowardly, panicky, schoolgirl screech. A bloody-poor-show screech. Corporal Hall didn't screech. What did he think of officers who did?

His cap fell off. As he reached for it, he caught a glimpse of the Zero's wing, coming straight for him, slicing through the air like a giant samurai sword. In a scintilla of time he saw himself slit neatly from skull to rectum, spread out in two matching halves like something at Mac Fisheries. Terror froze his brain. Christ, no, please no.... His eyes were tightly shut, pressed against his arm. He could smell the hairy warmth of his flesh. Every muscle cringed. Then suddenly, shockingly, the world became noise and heat and machinery howling, crumpling, rending, tearing, rolling itself into tightly sculptured junk. Scorching wind seared over Cornish's face. He scrambled a few terrified feet. Stopped. Opened his eyes.

'Strewth,' said a soldier with a freckled face.

The Japanese aircraft had cartwheeled across the road into the gully on the other side. Already some of the men were on their feet, hurrying over to have a look. Flames and black smoke vomited upward.

'Watch out!' someone yelled. 'It'll blow up!'

That's very true, Cornish thought numbly. He rubbed his eyes. He had a headache. Was it any wonder?

'You all right, sir?'

'Yes, thank you, Corporal.'

One thing about me, Cornish thought, is that I usually control my funk rather well. I can ask questions and answer questions. I create the illusion of being in control.

Hall said, 'Jap must have seen you was an officer, sir. Aimed 'is plane right at you, 'e did.'

'Nasty of him, wasn't it?'

Dusting himself off, Cornish told Hall to carry on. The corporal saluted. Keen type, Hall. What was he in civilian life? An undertaker? He looked the part with his long thin face and his grey eyes. Just the job in black suit and top hat. Cornish took a deep breath. Oh Lord, that smell. Roasting human. His left hand was still shaking a bit. Could one side of you be more frightened than the other? Press the hand firmly into the waist. Noël Cowardish but a lot better than a public display of the shakes. Next: set mouth in firm line to indicate keen interest in current goings-on. Hell.

There was a low half-muffled boom from the gully. Fresh

flames shot skyward. The troops shied back as if blown by the hot wind.

Cornish ordered himself to cross the road. He didn't want to go but it seemed necessary. The Zero was a horror of shattered metal and flame. The heat was intense; Cornish could bear to look only for an instant at a time, darting glances from behind a shielding hand. The transparent plastic of the cockpit canopy had darkened and ruptured but inside something could still be seen. Something huddled and crushed.

'Serves him bloody right,' said a Scot, shouldering his rifle with the air of having completed a job efficiently.

Cornish turned away. That was a bloody near thing, he thought. Probably the nearest thing yet. The nearest thing since it had all started, with the Jap landings at Kota Bharu and Patani and Singora at the beginning of December. And one of the all-too-few occasions on which the enemy had come off second best. Now the men were grinning, warmed by the entirely erroneous belief that they had scored a major victory by bringing down one plane. Every other man was claiming to have fired the all-important shot. As if it mattered....

Inside the Zero's cockpit, flesh and metal were fusing to form some unspeakable substance. Hard cheese, old man, Cornish said to the pilot. At some point in time, he thought, that disgusting looking mess was adored by its mother, regarded as the most delectable of creatures. Now even its mother would be repelled by the sight of it. Would she soon hear of her son's death? 'Gallant sacrifice ... on the sacred soil of battle ... for the Emperor ...' Undoubtedly the telegram would say all the right things; all such telegrams did. The wording was official, sacrosanct, having been drafted and redrafted and perused by endless committees of generals and admirals and politicians, all striving to capture just that right tone of sense of loss combined with pride and gratitude...

Rather like getting copy approved for an advertisement, Cornish thought.

He turned away from the wreck and took another deep breath. He felt calmer. Should he delegate some men to put out the flames? No. The plane could be left to burn itself out; the fire was safe in the gully. It was more important to get the men up the hill.

'Flipped across the ruddy road.'

'Miracle 'e didn't 'it no one.'

'Stupid sod.'

The British troops plodded up the hill. It had a fiendish incline. And the weather was no help. Bodies poured sweat until shirts and trousers became evil-smelling second skins. Men felt as if they were dissolving in the sodden heat.

Cornish tried to hold himself erect as he trudged. 'Nothing takes the heart out of the men as much as seeing their officers becoming slovenly and careless because of a spot of fatigue.' A moustachio'd major had drummed it into them in a Nissen hut somewhere deep in the heart of Essex. The hut had been dismally heated and rain had pattered on the steel roof and the major had droned on about how *he* had steadfastly refused to succumb to fatigue throughout the retreat to Dunkirk, though constantly harried by Hun planes...

The present returned with a shock. Rapidly Cornish scanned the sky. Thank God, there seemed to be no more Jap planes about.

'Hurry along, chaps.'

The men absorbed the words—and very sensibly ignored them. Cornish thought, If the poor sods ran up the hill at four minutes a mile, we'd still be telling them to hurry along.

He paused in the long, coarse grass beside the road and looked back to where the Zero was still burning furiously. Near the wreck stood the incongruous figure of Tom Byrne, Unofficial Padre. He wore his white robes; he held his pith helmet in one hand, his prayer book in the other. He must have been saying a few words for the immortal soul of the dead Jap pilot. Tom was always prepared, like a boy scout.

'Sir?'

Cornish turned. It was Sergeant Firmin; he saluted with unwonted haste. Not waiting for a response, he blurted out:

'Can you come up to the top of the hill, sir?'

'That's where I am going, Sergeant.'

'I know, sir. But quickly. Something's happened, sir. Something terrible.'

Cornish's stomach sagged with the dread of what Firmin might have to tell him. 'Well, what is it?'

Firmin lowered his voice. 'Sir, the Jap plane, it got the C.O.' He looked at Cornish as if fearful of telling him the rest. Then: 'It got Major Roberts and Major Dalton too.'

'Got them?' Cornish wiped the sweat from his eyes. He clenched his left hand. 'You mean they're dead?' It was easy to say, less easy to contemplate.

'I think the Second-in-Command and the Adjutant are dead, sir. And the Colonel is badly hurt. Really badly, sir.'

Oh my God. How the hell could such a thing happen? What stupidity? ... Cornish found himself becoming infuriated with Firmin, blaming him personally for the disaster.

'I think they were standing together, sir; a briefing. That was the trouble. The Jap came low, caught them unawares.'

'Is the M.O. with them?'

'Yes sir. And Major Kerr wants to see you as soon as possible.'

'Major Kerr?'

'Yes sir, I think he's in command now ... if the colonel ...'
'All right, Sergeant Firmin, I'm coming at once.'
'Yes sir.'
Cornish frowned. *Kerr?*

3

Major Ernest George Kerr stood on the spongy floor of the native hut, his feet exactly eighteen inches apart, his hands interlocked behind his back. The thumb of his right hand lay in the precise centre of the palm of his left; the fingers of his right hand lightly clasped the knuckles of his left. He had assumed the posture automatically; it was entirely natural to him; it enabled him to balance his body well and thus forget about it. He could stand stock-still for hours without undue fatigue: a useful ability, for in the course of more than a quarter of a century of military service a man spends an astonishing number of hours utterly motionless. It was in March of 1914 that Ernest George Kerr had taken the tram from Rochdale to Manchester and had joined the ranks of the Lancashire Fusiliers. He had been a singularly lithe and athletic youth. Now, in middle age, he still possessed a body of fine proportions. He had a massive, slightly jutting jaw, a thick nose and an aggressive set to his broad-lipped mouth. He was a rudely handsome man who exuded vigour. His eyes were deep brown beneath bushy brows; his hair was still thick but some grey now streaked the black.

Kerr watched as Gibbs, the M.O., worked on the Colonel. It was a waste of time and medical supplies. Kerr knew it and Gibbs knew it and perhaps even the Commanding Officer knew it. Kerr had seen many men die; he knew that waxen look when the body dies before the brain. No doubt about it: Lieutenant-Colonel Arthur Brigden was being posted upstairs.

A charming gentleman, the colonel, but in Kerr's private opinion a bit *too* bloody charming and gentlemanly. Beautifully bred for the Hunt, was the colonel, but all wrong for a savage, no-holds-barred war.

Through the open doorway Kerr watched the troops straggling by, dulled and exhausted by the climb up the hill. A sorry-looking lot, he thought; we're going to have our work cut out to win with them.

Tom Byrne hurried in, gasping, his thin face shiny with sweat. He glanced quickly around the small room and nodded to Kerr.

'Padre,' said Kerr, nodding in reply.

'Is there anything I can do?'

You'll need an extra-special prayer for this one, Kerr thought.

'Hullo, Tom,' said Gibbs, not looking up from his patient.

Outside, a 3-tonner clattered, steaming, into the centre of the *kampong*. The lorry's springs groaned under the weight of 50-pound boxes of .303 cartridges, tens of thousands of rounds for the riflemen's Lee-Enfields.

Thank Christ the plane didn't get *that*, Kerr thought as he strode out of the hut and yelled at the men to look bloody sharp about unloading the lorry. Faces, browned and blank, turned toward him; then, as they identified him, it was all furious flustered activity. Kerr sniffed. Gormless sods. Why did they always have to be ordered? Couldn't they see the urgency for themselves?

He stood for a moment and glared at the men as they worked. The full heat of the sun hit him, cutting easily through the thin fabric of his tropicals. He was aware of the heat but derived a certain satisfaction from refusing to react to it. No puffing and blowing for him. He had long ago accepted the fact that he, as a soldier, was destined to spend most of his time in places much too hot or much too cold for comfort. So to hell with thinking about comfort.

Watching the troops, Kerr told himself: You always wanted a command, didn't you, lad? Well, there it is. That lot. They look so fagged, a good stiff breeze would blow them all down. And they're scared silly of the enemy. They're all yours.

Cornish approached. Even hurrying in crumpled tropicals with a heavy revolver banging on his thigh, Cornish had a rich man's way of moving. An easiness. Quality lubrication. Kerr noted it with a sociological interest—then chided himself. It's hardly the time or place, Ernie.

'You wanted to see me, sir?'

'Aye.' Kerr inclined his head towards the hut. 'You heard about the colonel? He's in there. Roberts and Dalton are dead.'

'And the colonel?'

'He soon will be.'

'Oh, I see.' Cornish looked at the ground.

They walked back to the hut. As they entered, the colonel moved feebly; he was trying to say something. Kerr stooped over him.

'I'm here, sir. Don't worry. We'll soon have you up and about. In the meantime, have you any instructions...?'

The colonel's eyes closed again. His lips moved.

'Padre...'

'I'm here, my son,' said Tom Byrne softly.

'But I'm not a Catholic...'

'That's not important. Will you pray with me, my son?'

'I...'

'Lord have mercy...'

But the colonel's life had already spluttered foully out of him. His head rolled back, mouth gaping, upper dentures coming loose, obscenely, at the moment of death.

'He's gone,' said Gibbs, examining the colonel's eyes.

Told you, said Kerr to himself.

Tom's cropped head was bowed reverentially over the body.

Kerr turned and walked out into the sunlight. There was nothing more to be done for the C.O., except bury him. Trust the old bastard to use his last breath to discuss his religious denomination...

Cornish emerged, looking pale.

Kerr said, 'He was a good man and a good officer but we'll have to carry on without him.'

'Yes, sir,' said Cornish with little enthusiasm.

The troops glanced up at the two officers as they trudged by in sodden procession. By now the news would have reached every man, quickly, cruelly dousing the elation caused by the Zero's destruction.

'We want to organize a burial party,' said Kerr. 'Those men were senior officers and we're going to bury them with full honours whether the bloody Japs are coming or not. First, though, I'm thinking that you and I should have a look around. Get the lie of the land. This is a right good position we've got here, but we want to be sure we use it the right way. Has Broadbent got that wireless of his working yet?'

Cornish said he had no idea.

'Well, we'd better find out, hadn't we? It's important, bloody important.' Kerr squinted up at the high ground above the *kampong*. He waited for Cornish's protestation that Broadbent wasn't his responsibility therefore it was hardly reasonable to expect him to know whether the wretched man's wireless set was bloody well working or not working, etcetera, etcetera...

The protestation almost took form; you could *feel* it under construction. Then, abruptly, Cornish sent a man to find Broadbent.

Kerr smiled to himself.

The hill extended beyond the village in a series of slopes. A couple of larger-than-average huts stood on the highest point, overlooking the north slope. The élite lived up there, Kerr thought, the ones with all the brass. He wondered if they were hiding in the jungle with the other villagers, keeping out of sight until the foreign soldiers had gone.

'Let's get up there, lad. We'll have a good view of things.'

Climbing was punishing work in that heat and humidity. The sweat streamed out of you, oceans of it, until you looked as if you had been dipped in a vat of the stuff. Kerr reached the top first; Cornish followed, puffing.

'What's the matter? Warm, are you?'

'Strangely enough, I am a little.'

Kerr sniffed. 'Sarcasm doesn't become you.'

Cornish nodded, still breathing hard. 'Sorry, sir.'

Kerr lit his pipe and gazed over the vastness of the jungle. It seemed endless and yet the sea wasn't all that far to the east. Twenty-five miles, perhaps; by the look of it, it might have been twenty-five hundred. All around, the ground broke into jungle-covered hills. Ahead was the road leading down from the north. That was the way the Japs were coming. Rapidly. Below, the riflemen were stumbling about in their new positions. Confused as hell. Not knowing what sort of place they were in. Not knowing whether they would ever get out of it. And still far too docile. Sheep. Tame sheep. Too few of them and all of them insufficiently trained. And not very brilliantly led. Was that a fair statement? Kerr thought about it and nodded. Yes, a fair, accurate statement. He asked himself whether he could do better than Lieutenant-Colonel A. Brigden, M.C. Aye, Kerr thought, I can and I will.

'May I ask what our orders are, sir?'

'Our orders? Very simple and straightforward—which suits me because I'm a very simple and straightforward man. Occupy this position. And halt the enemy's progress.'

'Is that all?'

'Aye, that's it.'

Enthusiasm wasn't exactly bubbling out of Captain Cornish, Kerr noted—but then, was it ever? Something of a cold fish, was Captain Cornish. 'Reserved' was the polite description. Kept himself very much to himself. Wanted nothing less than to be One of the Boys. Kerr knew the type. Shy and rich. But reasonably intelligent, therefore useful.

Kerr puffed smoke out over the jungle. 'We don't know each other very well,' he said. 'But I need a 2 i/c or an Adjutant or anything you want to call yourself. My idea is that you're it. All right?'

Cornish looked away. 'To be frank, sir, I don't think you've made a particularly wise choice.'

'Why?'

'Very simply,' said Cornish, 'I've discovered that I'm not very brave. In fact, when I'm being shot at, I'm scared bloody stiff. I didn't know it until the first shots were fired. I'm not particularly proud of it, but there it is.'

'A lot of men are scared,' said Kerr. 'Shit-scared. But they carry on. You've been carrying on, haven't you?'

'Yes, I suppose I have.'

Kerr tamped the warm tobacco. He had made up his mind; he wasn't about to change it. 'You'll do, Cornish.'

'Very well, sir. Thank you.'

'Don't thank me. It's going to be a right sod of a job unless I miss my guess. But you seem to have a bit of a brain between your ears. You'll manage. We should make a good team, the two of us. We're different. I came up from the ranks, you know.'

'So I heard.'

'They tell me you're an Oxford man.'

'Yes, sir.'

'You're lucky then. You had advantages. You're from London, I understand. You may have observed from the lilt in my voice that I'm from farther north.'

'Yes, sir, I had noticed.'

'I thought you might have done. I'm a very competent soldier, Cornish.'

'I beg your pardon, sir?'

'I was saying what a competent soldier I am. I said it to try and calm your fears a bit. It's also true. So you needn't think everything's lost because most of Battalion H.Q. is gone. I'm just as good as any of them.'

A bleak smile touched Cornish's lips. 'I'm glad to hear it.'

'I thought you might be ... Do you think we can stop the Japs?'

Cornish was taken aback. 'Stop them? I don't know ... I hope so ... but I don't know.'

'Why don't you know?'

'Well ... to be honest, I don't think we're a match for the Japs. That's rather defeatist, I suppose, but you asked the question. They seem to be professionals at all this and we're such amateurs—except for you and a few others, of course.'

'Thanks very much, I'm sure.'

'Frankly, I feel something of an imposter wearing this uniform.'

'You *are* honest.'

'It's one of my few virtues.'

'What's your opinion of this position?'

'It's a fine defensive position, sir. But what worries me is how easily we could be surrounded ... and cut off.'

'Aye, you've got a point there. But right now we've got

other things to think about. Mr Johnny Jap is on his way. We're going to give him a nasty shock when he gets here. This is a right sod of a place to take. I don't know when I've seen one worse. Look at the road. It follows the gentlest part of the slope; it's steep on either side and there's a gully at the bottom. Christ, it's as bad as that place, you know, where that feller held off all the bloody Persians.'

'Thermopylae.'

'Aye, that's it. What was he called?'

'Leonidas.'

'Good. You didn't waste your time at Oxford.'

Kerr himself had left school at fourteen, having already spent two years working half days at the mill where his father was a piecer bent over a spinning mule, his feet bare on the hot timber floor. His father had died of spinner's cancer, an old and wasted man at forty-three. It was unfair, Kerr often thought, but wasn't almost everything in life unfair? So why did the unfairness of things maintain its ability to surprise and dismay? Why wasn't everyone in the entire world inured to it by now?

'They tell me your family is very important in the advertising profession.'

'I wouldn't call it a profession, sir. It's a business, pure and simple.'

'A business, then. *Are* you very important in it?'

'Fairly important, I suppose.'

'How important?'

'Well, we *are* considered one of the three principal agencies in the country.'

'Very nice too. You're lucky. You have something worth going home to.'

Cornish nodded rather curtly, clearly not relishing talk of the family empire. Kerr was amused and might have pursued the subject if Corporal Broadbent had not come puffing up the slope. He was a thin man with cavernous cheeks. He saluted damply. 'I'm sorry, sir, but the wireless still isn't workin' right. I'm transmittin' all right—leastways I think I am—but there's nothin' comin' in. No signal, no nothin'.'

'What can you do about it, lad?'

'Not a hell of a lot, sir, to tell the truth. I got no spares... We've had a lot of overheating trouble. I've rigged up a sky-wave—won't get far on rod with all this rubber and jungle about.'

Kerr nodded. 'Aye, well, do your best, that's all we ask. It's important that we tell Brigade we're here.'

'Yes, sir. I'll keep tryin'.'

As Broadbent went slipping and slithering down the slope, Kerr said, 'There's our first problem, Cornish: we're out of contact with Brigade. What do you suggest?'

'Where is Brigade, sir?'

'I wish I knew.'

Cornish stared. 'You're not serious.'

'I fear I am.'

'Christ.'

'Aye, it's a right bugger, isn't it? We don't know whether they're over that way or over that way or even over that way. They might even be north of us for all I know, but I very much doubt it.'

Cornish said, 'I suggest we send out runners, south, east and west. In the meantime Corporal Broadbent had better keep on transmitting in the hope that something gets through.'

Kerr smiled. 'At last we agree on something, Captain Cornish.'

23

4

They buried the colonel and the two majors shortly before sunset. Kerr was crisply attired in neat tunic and well-pressed campaign trousers. Tom Byrne stood beside him and read the deceased officers into the next world. Nature provided a suitably sombre accompaniment. The skies darkened; threatening clouds piled one upon the other; in the distance thunder rumbled. It wouldn't be long before there would be rain. And Japs.

The makeshift coffins—they had been knocked together that afternoon with lumber torn from ammunition boxes—were lowered into the sticky Malayan soil. The guard of honour fired the traditional three volleys, said, by those who delved into such matters, to symbolize the Trinity. Live bullets were used. Kerr had insisted. There was to be no cheapening of the ceremony just because a few ruddy Orientals were coming, he had declared. Loudly.

The troops stood in a large semi-circle, glumly watching yet another scene in the pageant of catastrophes that had been their war to date. The colonel was gone; so were Majors Roberts and Dalton. Now it was all up to Major Kerr. Bags of bull. But had he any brains? Had any regular, they wondered.

Ninety per cent of the men were conscripts between the ages of nineteen and twenty-four, directed by H.M. Government to serve for The Duration of the Present Emergency. Only a fraction of them had ever been abroad before and, for most of those, 'abroad' meant a day-trip to Calais. Now they found themselves in a bewilderingly foreign land. They had arrived only a matter of weeks before, many of them vague about whom they were supposed to be defending and against whom. Now, after a couple of months of confused retreat, they were grim and jittery. As far as they were concerned the Japs were welcome to the whole lousy peninsula and good luck to them.

Kerr stood with his hands on his hips.

'We've just said farewell to three gallant officers,' he declared. Slowly he walked, looking straight into men's eyes. For what seemed an eternity he said nothing else—the major knew the dramatic value of total silence. Then: 'They died as I know they would have wanted to die: on the field of battle. And we're the ones who are left to carry on. Which is just exactly what we're going to do. You may not be aware of this, lads—' he gave them a sharp smile—'but we're going to give the Japs a bloody good hiding when they come! Oh yes, believe me, we are. The little buggers are going to wish they'd never run into us!'

As he listened, Cornish realized that Kerr had gone into the wrong profession. He should have gone on the stage; he was a splendid actor.

The bamboo floor complained squeakily as the officers filed in. There were eight: two captains, three full lieutenants and three seconds. Dispirited and dishevelled young men in sweat-stained tropicals.

'I'm afraid there aren't any chairs,' said Cornish. 'The former occupants must have taken them when they left.'

The officers nodded gravely as if absorbing useful intelligence. They stood with their arms folded across their chests.

'Major Kerr will be here in a moment.'

More nods. The officers were as cheerless as their men.

And just as bewildered. Good lads, of course, but with hardly a couple of dozen years' service between the lot of them. Poor devils, they were all that was left of the establishment of thirty-three officers who, according to War Office dictum, were required to lead the 753 N.C.O.s and men of a rifle battalion of a British Army regiment of the line into battle against the King's enemies.

What a balls-up, Cornish thought bitterly.

Everyone snapped to attention as Kerr bustled in, brisk and bright, like a stockbroker anticipating a profitable day. The floor sagged anew. Kerr glared at it. It held.

'Good afternoon, gentlemen.' He gazed at each man for perhaps two seconds. He was no taller than most of them but he was burlier and his presence was huge. When he spoke he seemed to stress the Lancashire in his voice as if it pleased him to remind these admirably educated young gentlemen that he was a plain north-country lad. And proud of it. And in command.

'We've not got much time so I'll not take much,' he said. 'I intend this unit—I'll not call it a battalion any more—to be fully operational by the time the Japs come, because for your information we're going to beat the shit out of them. Do I make myself clear?' He produced a crude but adequate map of the locality drawn in blue-black ink on the back of a police poster. He fastened it to the *atap* wall with a straightened safety-pin. 'A bird's-eye view of this hill,' he said. 'Here's the road coming in from the north. The Japs are using it at this very moment. I reckon they're about here. And here we are. Facing them. Here's the village. Now, the Japs could attack us from several different directions. And at one and the same time. But the terrain is against them. You all climbed up that slope; you know what a sod it is. But it's even worse on the other sides. The east and west are bloody terrible and the south is just about out of the question unless you're a fucking mountain goat. By the way, the M.O. is setting up his A.D.S. over there. All right, any questions so far?' He peered at the officers, his great jaw defying any of them to doubt his logic. 'It's no use trying to hang on to the old battalion organization,' he said. 'You're the only company and platoon commanders left. So what I intend to do is divide the unit into sections. We'll call the biggest one North Section because it will be holding the north face of the hill. Captain Milne will be in command. On the east and west faces...'

Cornish looked at his boots. It sounded horribly like the orders for a last stand, ruthlessly discarding the intricate organization of the battalion: the assembly of rifle companies, each with precisely 5 officers, 119 O.R.s; the platoons of 1 officer, 36 men; the specialist sections: anti-aircraft, signals, motor transport, administration ... the whole organism wielding an arsenal of 717 rifles, 42 sub-machine-guns, 50 Brens, 4 Twin-Brens, 47 pistols, 24 anti-tank rifles, 6 3-inch mortars, 16 2-inch mortars ... Once he had learnt the whole thing by heart: 5 officers and 50 men in Battalion H.Q., armed with 11 pistols, 42 rifles, 2 sub-machine-guns and 1 Bren... In Company H.Q., 8 officers and 248 men... Endless reams of numbers that now meant precisely nothing because the battalion no longer existed. But perhaps it hadn't really existed since Benhang. There, it had been a nightmare of panic, men blazing wildly in every direction, killing each other in mistake for the enemy. No order, no organization. Only the frantic desire to fight off the Japs long enough to permit a scurrying away to safety. Men had run—Cornish had seen them—and some had thrown their rifles away to aid their flight. God knows what had happened to those men. Perhaps some had slunk back and rejoined their comrades; others were by now carcasses rotting in the jungle. Sergeant-major Freeman had died at

Benhang. Hit in the chest, he had toppled over backwards. His helmet fell off and rolled away. With some surprise, Cornish had noted that Freeman had only a fringe of snow-white hair left on his head. His was an old man's head. What was Freeman doing here? He should have been at home, playing with his grandchildren.

Kerr was talking about trenches, about organizing shift work so that the digging could go on all night.

'Any questions?'

Yes, I have a question, said Cornish without speaking. My question is: Major Kerr, are you really as happy as you look? You have the profoundly satisfied air of a man who is realizing an ambition of long standing. Is that it? Are you happy because at long last you are in command? I suspect that is it, Major Kerr. I also suspect that your happiness is quite undampened by the distressingly strong possibility of defeat. Or death. Or both.

You sound like George Formby, he thought, but I have to admit it: you do have a way with you.

It was night. Darkness fell in the sudden, startling way of the east. Men strained their eyes looking into the blackness of the jungle, searching for the Japs. They were coming; everyone knew that; but when? How much time was left? How much time to prepare for them? And might they attack from a totally unexpected direction? Clever little sods, the Japs, you had to give them their due. And they weren't all short-sighted and scared of the dark, as everyone was so bloody fond of saying—before everyone found out the awful truth about them.

'There's not enough shovels, sir.'

'Do you suggest I indent England for some more?'

'No sir, sorry sir, but I wanted to tell you, sir.'

'Very well, you have told me.'
'Yes, sir.'
Cornish sighed. 'Can't the chaps use their bayonets to cut the earth into chunks so that the men with shovels can simply pick up the chunks.'
'Ah. Yes, we'll try that, sir. It might work.'
'All right. Carry on.'
'Yes, sir.'
A sweaty salute. Boots slithering on the soft muck. Shouted commands to deploy bayonets, for Christ's sake, use your loafs....
Cornish walked along the road, along the rows of labouring, cursing, sweating men. It had rained briefly. Now it was still; the air was heavy and damp. The men seemed to be making the devil of a racket—and every sound was an urgent signal to the Japanese: We are here, ahead of you, in moderate strength and in our customary state of utter confusion.
A small Scot swore foully as he cut into the earth with his bayonet. Everyone from Churchill down was a target for his ire.
Cornish listened for a few moments before moving on. Was it a good sign, a man swearing so vehemently? Did it signal a return of Fighting Spirit?
Men's bodies glistened damply as they heaved boxes of Bren ammunition, each containing precisely 1,248 rounds (a count determined at the factory by weighing the boxes before putting the lids on).
Thank God we've got a fair amount of ammo, Cornish thought.
'Hullo, David.'
It was Tom Byrne. His grubby white robes looked ghost-like in the gloom. He was bareheaded. And smiling, as usual.

Cornish said, 'I was just thanking your boss for something.'

'My boss?'

'I was saying, "Thank God we've lots of ammo".'

'I'm delighted you two have established communications.'

'Ah, but I've had no reply yet.'

Tom chuckled. An ugly man, Tom, but attractive. His nose was too long and his chin too pointed, but then his mouth was uncommonly gentle and his eyes warm and very blue. He could have been any age from thirty to sixty. His closely cropped hair was grey but his face was unlined. He was an American, a Jesuit priest, whose mission had been demolished by Japanese artillery. As the battalion had withdrawn from the burning village, so had Tom. Quite naturally, it seemed, he had taken the place of Captain the Reverend Arnold P. Binns, who had vanished in the explosion of an ammunition truck near Ipoh.

Cornish said, 'I'm organizing some runners, Tom. They're going to try to get through to the main force and tell them that we're here. It might be as well if you went along with them.'

'Do you want me to go along with them?'

'It's going to be nasty when the Japs arrive. You're a civilian; there's no reason for you to get yourself mixed up in it.'

'I'd rather stay if it's OK with you.'

'Think about it.'

'I just did.'

'It's your funeral, old boy.'

'You have a persuasive charm, David.'

'I'm merely stating the facts.'

'I'll stay.'

'Very well. The men will be pleased. But don't go around converting all the poor sods to Catholicism;

they've got enough trouble as it is.'
'You're an evil man, Captain Cornish.'
'I know. You keep telling me.'

The explosive was carefully placed in slits cut in the ground by bayonet. Two sticks nestled together, every five or six feet. The dynamite was commercial stuff commandeered from an abandoned tin mine. Not nearly as effective as proper anti-personnel mines—but considerably better than nothing. The set-up was simple: detonators were fastened to the sticks—one to every two sticks because there was a shortage of detonators—and electric light wire connected the detonators to the starter coils in the engines of the three lorries.

A hundred men were assigned to the road job. Laboriously they dug a twenty-foot by twenty-foot cube out of the earth. Then they bridged it with a network of branches on which they placed a layer of gravel and stones.

'We think our wireless messages are getting through,' said Cornish, hoping he sounded confident. 'But we're not absolutely sure, you see, because we can't receive any messages.'

Before him, six riflemen nodded suspiciously, wondering what the hell they had let themselves in for. Volunteering was chancy, bloody chancy.

Cornish went on: 'We want to be quite sure that H.Q. knows we're in position here. That's why I asked for volunteers. I want the six of you to divide yourselves into three teams of two men each. Then, well, off you go. One team east, one west, one south. All you have to do is tell any British forces you find that we're here, on this hill. The reason we're sending three teams is pretty obvious, I think.

Frankly, we're not at all sure where the British forces are. All right, any questions?'

'Sir,' said Private Martin Soper, 'what if we run into Australian forces? Is it all right to tell them?'

Patiently, Cornish told him, yes, it was all right to tell the Australians. Indian forces, too.

'Me and George Latimer are one team,' said Private Soper. 'Bags we go south.'

Cornish ordered about twenty trees on the north slope to be cut down: a fiendish job at night. The men couldn't see what they were doing and were scared stiff the bloody things might fall on them. Once the trees were cut down, soggy, oozing things alive with maggots, they had to be hauled up to the road. Ropes were looped round the leaden trunks, and while those up on the road heaved, the others pushed until their eyeballs started to pop. Their boots slipped on the treacherous slope and they scrambled desperately away before the falling trunk crushed them along with the maggots.

Whose sodding idea was this anyway? The men worked through the night, cursing maggots, cursing tree-trunks and above all cursing Cornish.

An Army in retreat loses its spirit; it ebbs away at an almost predictable rate: so many miles backwards, so much spirit lost. The one cure is to turn and face the enemy; only then can spirit be regained.

On the hill, the British troops swore and groaned as they sliced six-foot-deep trenches in the heavy soil. They hacked through iron-hard tree-trunks; they sweated gallons as they hauled boxes full of ammunition. They became groggy with fatigue. One man chopped two fingers off another man's hand because his eyes had closed involuntarily as he swung the axe. Another man broke a leg when he blundered sleepily into a freshly dug trench. Everyone cursed but everyone worked hard. No one had to be told how urgent it all was. There was a feeling, still not matured but beginning to take full form, that things were being half-decently organized for once; someone up top was doing a bit of thinking for a change. The men sensed that this time they stood some chance of meeting the enemy prepared. God knows what would happen ... but it had become a habit not to think too far ahead, anyway....

At last the sun appeared, first just a glow behind the hills, then an enormous fan of pink and gold that touched the tips of the tallest jungle trees. Immediately below, it was still night; for a short time the hill seemed to be floating on a sea of black.

It was dawn, the cool part of any Malayan day, the air fresh and dry, vegetation smelling clean and wholesome. On the hill, every fifth man had been on look-out duty for two hours. The rest of the men were slumped against breastwork and trench floor, lost in exhausted sleep.

The sun slid into full view. With it came the heat.

Cornish adjusted the binoculars' focus. The waving trees loomed. Innocent enough. No half-hidden Japs. Where was the road? Ah, yes, a little to the right. All quiet too. But were the Japs around the next corner, thousands upon thousands of them, tumbling all over one another in their grinning eagerness to get to grips with the enemy?

Oh, do belt up, he told his imagination.

'Nothing doing, sir,' he reported to Kerr.

'All right,' said Kerr, 'then let's go and have a brandy.'

'A brandy? I haven't had breakfast yet.'

'Breakfast is just another dinner if you've been up all night.'

5

Kerr poured a few gills into two enamel mugs. He had liberated two bottles of Rémy Martin from a planter's abandoned house, along with a dozen bottles of Tiger beer. The beer had long since gone, so had one bottle of cognac, but half the second bottle remained.

'If you're going to loot,' said Kerr, 'you may as well loot good quality stuff as the cheap stuff.' He saw Cornish glance at the label and nod. Mr Cornish didn't have to be told that it was good stuff; he knew; undoubtedly he had grown up with Rémy Martin and the very best of every other bloody thing.

'The runners away?'

'Yes, sir. I tried to get Tom Byrne to go with them but he refused—'

Kerr stared. 'You did what?'

'I tried to get Tom Byrne to go—'

'What the hell for?'

'It seemed a sensible move.'

'A sensible move? To send off our one and only padre? That's not sensible, that's bloody daft! We need a padre! The men will fight better if there's a padre around.'

'I know, sir, but Tom is a civilian and an American....'

Kerr shook his head. 'Christ, I don't care if he's a bloody Abyssinian. He's a padre. That's all that matters. He'll tell the men to fight the good fight with all their bloody might. Therefore he's useful. You see?'

Flushed, Cornish said that he saw.

Bloody amazing what they don't teach at Oxford, Kerr thought. He said, 'What do you think of the officers?'

'The officers?' Cornish ran a hand through his hair.

Kerr could imagine him thinking: Can't the bastard see that I'm tired out? Can't he pick another time to discuss personnel? Kerr smiled to himself. 'An intelligent and capable officer but tends to react somewhat emotionally when under duress.' Signed, E. G. Kerr (Major).

'I'd be interested in your opinion.'

Cornish nodded and stared bleakly at the *atap* floor. 'Sir, in brief, I think they are able and certainly they're willing. But they lack experience. And that includes me.'

'Go on.'

'Bob Milne is a good type. A Gunner, as you know. Unfortunately, no artillery. Perhaps not the most original thinker in the world, but extremely conscientious. And not easily rattled. Johnson is a pretty good fellow. At least, he looks fine, which is something, I suppose, but I really don't know him that well. Morton was with me when the Japs cut the road behind us. He handled himself very well. Charles White is a clever chap; reads Plato in ancient Greek. Porson appears to be perpetually randy; I've never heard him mention anything but women. And I'm afraid I know even less about the others,' he added with a shrug.

'You keep yourself too much to yourself,' said Kerr. It amused him to watch the reaction: the flush on the young noble's brow; a tightening of the lip. No doubt he was making a mental note to remember this absurdity for the club: 'Imagine, there we were in the middle of the jungle and this silly old sweat of a major grandly informed me that I hadn't been keeping up with my social obligations!' That should raise a princely guffaw from the esteemed members. Kerr said, 'It's important to know as much as you can about your men and your brother officers.' He

35

yawned expansively. 'I think one of us should be awake at all times.' Predictably, Cornish's mouth hardened; he thought he knew what was coming next, so it amused Kerr to say: 'You have a couple of hours now.' Muttered thanks in response. 'Aye, it is good of me,' said the major, smiling to himself.

He watched Cornish stretch out on the floor and close his eyes. At once he looked younger. About twenty.

Brian's age, thought Kerr; the age he would have been.

He frowned away the thought. He didn't want to think of Brian. It still hurt like bloody hell. He forced his mind to return to the present. He reviewed, one by one, the steps he had taken to prepare for the enemy. He had done well—far more than most officers could have done under the circumstances. And yes, Cornish had helped. Cornish, for all his cold-potatoes personality, did possess a brain. He had ideas. And, Kerr reflected, I've been clever enough to use them.

Kerr was eighteen years old when he first went into battle. He stood behind a wall of sandbags, more terrified of messing his trousers and disgracing himself than of the enemy. His fingers were ice cold. He had a very real fear of dropping his rifle when the time came to move. In front of him, at eye level, sand was trickling from a torn bag. Private Kerr reflected on its close resemblance to the sand he remembered on the beach at Scarborough. Could it actually be sand on which he had walked with bare feet? The thought occupied him for a few nerve-grinding moments. He pictured the boarding house with the notice in the hall about wet swimming costumes and sand, the tinted portrait of Queen Victoria and the scene from the 1908 Olympic Games, the odd smell of seaweed and cabbage. It drizzled for two of the three August Bank holiday weekend days. And the meals were tasteless and unsubstantial. But Mr and Mrs Kerr persisted in declaring how well they were eating and how the weather was on the mend, without question. They had looked forward to that rotten little holiday so much that nothing, not the lodgings, not the food, not the weather, could be permitted to spoil it. They chose to pretend rather than admit and regret. As he stood on duckboards in an advance trench, Kerr realized that only poor people would put up with it; if you had brass you didn't have to; you told them where to insert their watery cabbage and you moved into the Grand. 'Patient now, lads, it won't be long,' said the sergeant, gruffly kind. He looked old enough to have been at Balaclava. A far better leader of men than most of the generals, he artfully implied to the young soldiers that they were *anxious* to go over the top.

Then Kerr was scrambling over the sandbags, laden with fifty pounds of arms and equipment. The man on his right dropped with a squeak of pain. He half vanished in the mud. Kerr's boots slithered on the stuff; he almost fell. Ahead, through blowing smoke, he saw the winking red lights of machine-guns. Spandaus, Parabellums. In front of him a man threw up his hands and plunged forward in death as if diving into a pool. He saw a man cut in half by machine-gun bullets; the top half of him was sliced from his waist and fell off sideways. His hand still clutched his rifle. A bullet hit Kerr's cap—it was before the days of steel helmets—and jerked it forward over his eyes. For a moment he was blinded, but he kept running. With his free hand, he quickly pushed the cap back on his head. He almost collided with an officer, a lieutenant with a pinkish moustache and frightened eyes. The lieutenant's Savile-Row-tailored tunic was spattered with red-brown mud. Get down! Get down! In a motion simultaneously urgent and effeminate, the officer flapped his hand at anyone who could see him. Kerr took his advice. And he landed flat on the mud the instant the lieutenant was blown to smithereens. He simply vanished. Kerr reflected that if he hadn't dived when he had, he would in all probability have vanished also. The mud was like glue. And it seemed to afford little safety. The air above Kerr whirred with German bullets. He tried to bury himself, wriggle out of sight, become invisible to those murderous gunners. The bastards were aiming at him, personally! Any second, they'd get him! He hadn't a chance! And suddenly, as if he had just come to his senses, he realized that there was only one course of action open to him: Get out of this, Ernie Kerr. Bugger off home to Rochdale. You're bloody daft if you stay here a moment longer! You'll be *dead*! Almost involuntarily it seemed, he dragged his left arm out of the muck and began to turn himself. And promptly found himself face to face with the sergeant. A lean finger indicated the whereabouts of the enemy line. The sergeant said, 'You wouldn't be forgettin' that the Germans are over there, now would you?'

Kerr smiled, remembering. For the umpteenth time he wondered what might have happened if that old sergeant had not been there, at that moment. Would he have turned tail? Desertion In The Face Of The Enemy? No, he told himself, as he had told himself so many times before, I know I would have come to my senses in time. What the hell happened to the old sergeant? And why, Kerr pondered, do I call him 'old' when he was probably no older than I am now. I don't feel old, he thought, but, Christ, I do feel tired. He rubbed his forehead and informed himself that he was not the least bit tired; he was in fact as fresh as a bridegroom the first time on the first night ... Was it really necessary for either him or Cornish to be awake at all times? Wouldn't do any harm, really, to have forty winks ... His eyes were sticky and heavy and warm like fresh bread baking in the oven and the kitchen gloriously hot and stuffy, wholesomely smelly ... and a spare man in a collarless shirt wearing trousers too big around the middle held up by braces fraying at the rust-pitted metal clips ... a man coughing and grinning at the same time, apologetically, sorry about making so much noise and talking endlessly about soon shaking 'it' and feeling 'champion' again....

Anger snapped him back to consciousness. His fists were clenched and his heart pounded, shaking his body. But he had to think for a moment to recall the reason for his anger. Memories didn't fight fair; they lay in wait and ambushed you when your guard was down. He shook his head and stretched his shoulder muscles. Cornish was breathing regularly in deep—and no doubt dull—sleep.

The blue-black-ink map still adorned the wall. Its graceless lines depicted sections full of living men, a structure of logic and reason dedicated to killing. It was a good, businesslike map; 9 out of 10 at Tactical Defence School. Would the late colonel have approved? Kerr sniffed. Who gave a shit what the colonel would have approved? He stroked his chin. He needed a shave. Hester was always complaining about his beard no matter how frequently and closely he shaved. It made a rash on her cheek, she said, and it didn't take any great feat of imagination for anybody to guess what a young lady had been doing to get such a rash on her cheek. *That* sort of rash was caused by one thing and one thing only. Kerr had told her that it was impossible to make love with any gusto at all without the faces touching—unless of course she was willing to try some of the more exotic approaches in which the faces hardly came within yards of one another. Much blushing and shying-away. He was a naughty, naughty man to suggest anything of the sort. Kerr yawned. A very comfortable woman, Hester, he thought. Lovely breasts with chubby big nipples the colour of unvarnished cedar. But too many inhibitions. Too *nice*.

At forty, she still liked to think of herself as the Untouched English Rose. Daft, a woman her age. No wonder her first husband died; poor sod was probably bored to death. On the other hand, he thought, he did leave her very nicely provided for. Very nicely.

As he put on the fresh shorts and shirt that McGregor had laid out, he reflected that in a few years he might not care two hoots for Hester's sexual limitations; he would probably have some of his own.

Also, he thought, there's a damn good chance that you won't have any future whatsoever. In that case, you won't have to worry your silly head about marrying Hester or not marrying her.

Being a professional soldier, Kerr had often considered the possibility of sudden death. He had seen death at close quarters; it was no stranger. There was that first time over the top when the bullet had hit his cap. Six months later a hand grenade had fallen at his feet but had failed to explode. A transport truck had taken a direct hit from a 100-kilo H.E. bomb ninety seconds after he had clambered out, laden with rifle and kit. Traversing machine-guns had sliced men down on his left and right but had left him unharmed. One thought of such things and one thanked someone or something. Death was the possibility-but-not-probability, about as likely as a promotion to Percival's staff.

He put his pipe and pouch into his left-hand pocket, his fob-watch, his first-aid pack and a box of Swan Vestas into his right. Into his left breast pocket went his paybook; he put his glasses (hated symbols of the passage of time) into his right breast pocket snug in their imitation crocodile-hide case. He strapped his revolver belt around his waist and put on his cap. Where was his chrome-steel mirror ('Unbreakable! The Soldier's Friend!')? Ah, yes, tucked down beside the socks. He studied his reflection and was moderately pleased. Cap squarely over eyebrows, bush-shirt trim on shoulders, belt untwisted. He slipped the mirror in his left breast pocket behind his paybook (everyone knew someone who knew someone whose life had been saved by having just such a mirror in just such a spot) and went outside.

Heat enveloped him. To the north the road still seemed peaceful and deserted. No sounds of approaching armies, nothing but the noises of the jungle and the curses of men labouring to dig trenches in the unwilling soil. It was odd, he thought, how during the long retreat the men seemed to lose their identities; they became just so many units of humanity to organize and shuffle and order and scold. Now they were becoming individuals once more: the Cockney with the apparently inexhaustible store of dirty stories; the Kentish man with the remarkably simian features; the Liverpudlian with the explosive laugh; the corporal with the huge bottom; the private with the weird ears; the one with the bouncy walk; the one who looked like a bank clerk; the one who looked like Fagin; the one who looked like Robert Taylor; the one who looked too young; the one who was totally bald at twenty; the one who giggled; the one who never smiled.... The typical mixture. Presumably the Japs had their equivalents. All armies did. And an officer's job was to get the best out of them. The most efficient way was to make them believe that they wanted to give of their best, which on the face of it was absurd; yet men could be persuaded to suffer horribly and die with a kind of willingness. The way to accomplish this miracle was not to talk of King and country and democracy and freedom. The way was to convince them that the average courage of the unit was slightly higher than the individual's courage. Soldiers could never tell one another what they truly thought of the battle. If they did, and discovered that each was as terrified and confused and frustrated as the next, then they would all pack up and go home.

He wondered where the rest of the British Army had vanished to. And the Aussies. And the Indians. Where the hell were they all? In Singapore? Or on a boat for Blighty? No wonder Broadbent couldn't raise anyone with that blunderbuss of a wireless set of his; there was no one to raise; everyone had gone home.

It was a disquieting thought, to be squashed rapidly.

Perhaps, he thought, the whole idea is to let the Japs get well down the peninsula, then close in behind them. Surround them. Cut them off. Annihilate them. The thought pleased him. Surely there was such a plan in the works somewhere, surely all those highly paid generals were of *some* value; surely the Japs weren't suddenly *that* good and the British *that* bad.

A patriotic man, Kerr resented the Japanese success in Malaya. Every mile the little bastards had advanced was an insult to British arms. It was high time the sods were taught a lesson. Never had Kerr questioned the moral justification of the British presence in Malaya; he was of the opinion that without the British, Malaya would be a bloody shambles. The British had brought order and prosperity, now they were defending the place. And what happened? Half the Malays collaborated with the Japs, telling them where the British were positioned and in what strength. Four days before, a middle-aged Malay had been brought in as a suspected collaborator. The man had pleaded innocence. But he hadn't convinced Kerr—who had had him shot without further ado. The incident hadn't crossed his mind since. Eliminating a collaborator troubled his conscience no more than did stepping on a snake.

Around him the trees were dense and lush, their broad leaves stirring gently in the breeze. Peaceful and languid.

But sweaty. No wonder the planters spent half their waking hours downing *stengahs*. Kerr had no use for the planters; in pre-invasion days they had complained to the Governor every time the army had organized any military exercises —soldiers damaged rubber plants and frightened the workers, they said. Now, thought Kerr with some satisfaction, the silly buggers are only too bloody happy to see soldiers—as long as they're not Jap soldiers.

He stared.

Rapidly his fingers unbuttoned his breast-pocket flap. He slipped his glasses on.

'Jesus,' he breathed.

Little black dots on the road. Metallic ants, moving along from the north. Two of them. A puff of dust above each one. Light tanks, no doubt, probably Type 95 jobs. They were Japs, obviously, for there weren't any British tanks in Malaya. Some cretin had decided that Malaya wasn't tank country; anyone could *see* that it wasn't tank country.

Anyone except the Japs, that is.

6

The tanks stopped a mile from the hill. They were grey and brown and their turret hatches were open and men's heads protruded from them. Very casual and unafraid, the men studied the hill through binoculars, their elbows resting on the 14-mm. thick steel of the turrets, the great barrels of the 37-mm. guns jutting out like enormous phalli.

The tanks were stationary for ten minutes, then the two commanders exchanged words, nodded. The tanks rumbled into motion: forward then into reverse, bouncing on the rough ground at the roadside. Finally, like noisy behemoths, they turned and rumbled off the way they had come.

A twin-engined aircraft appeared and flew about half a mile east of the hill then turned and angled to the south. Another turn brought it sweeping over the road.

'There's a Nip in the air today,' said Kerr loudly.

The men nearby grinned. A couple of men fired their rifles at the plane and had their names taken for wasting ammo.

The aircraft turned again and went off to look at the other hills. Cornish kept watching, hoping for a wall of anti-aircraft fire which would reveal the presence of an enormously powerful, ingeniously concealed friendly force nearby. He watched in vain. Presently the plane headed away to the north. It seemed a lifetime since any British aeroplanes had been seen. A Blenheim limping home with smoke trailing despondently from one engine: a flight of

Buffalos rising bravely to meet the foe and not returning. He told himself that at that very moment squadrons of Spitfires and Hurricanes were doubtless on their way north to wrest control of the air from the Japanese.

'Look!'

'Shit!'

All eyes snapped to the road. A string of vehicles. And men. Some of the men on bicycles, noisy clattering things with naked wheel rims because the tyres had rotted away in the fetid air.

Milne came bounding along, a whistle leaping energetically on a string around his neck.

'The Japs have arrived, David!'

'Yes, I noticed.'

An odd thing about Milne, Cornish suddenly observed, was that when he spoke only his jaw seemed to be involved; the rest of his face was apparently disinterested.

Milne moved on to organize men already organized. Orders, rapid and staccato, snapped from his ventriloquist's-dummy jaw. Men jammed steel helmets on their sweating heads and reached for their rifles. Webbings and slings, once blanco'd and babied, were now dark with filth.

The Japanese were purposeful-looking soldiers. There were Lord only knows how many lines of them, cycling or marching, choking the narrow road, a military tidal wave. Cornish swallowed. His mouth was sour with fear. I should have developed a taste for it by now, he thought.

'I see we have company.'

Kerr was examining the enemy through binoculars.

'Care to have a look?'

'Thank you.'

The Japanese were wiry men, some in shorts, some in breeches with puttees. They wore steel helmets or caps in a variety of colours, khaki, grey or brown. Captured British army three-tonners trundled along beside them in clouds of dust.

Officers stood beside the road in busy little groups and studied the hill before them. One officer pointed to it as he spoke to another; both men laughed with some gusto.

'They're thinking it over,' said Kerr. 'Wondering whether to come straight up the road and hope for the best or perhaps try it around the sides. They're going to get a bloody shock when they see how steep those sides are!'

He laughed loudly.

Milne and Morton chuckled too. Cornish didn't see anything funny in the sight of umpteen heavily armed Japanese. Trepidation rumbled about inside him like a badly digested meal.

Kerr spoke to a private with slightly protruding eyes. 'What do you think of them, lad?'

A nervous laugh. 'Not a hell of a lot, sir.'

'Nor me,' said Kerr. 'I'm glad we feel the same way about the buggers.' He pretended not to be able to identify the soldier's accent, evincing much delight when told the boy was from Newcastle. 'A Geordie! Of course! Grand!' It was well done; it sounded genuine. The soldier was pleased. And that was all that really mattered.

Cornish sighed. The all-important lubricant of war wasn't oil, after all; it was bullshit. Kerr knew it. The rough-hewn charm, the grave nod, the sudden grin. All bull. But men responded. It couldn't be denied. 'Ignore the officer togs,' Kerr seemed to say. 'I'm really one of *you*; I'm not one of those toffee-nosed lah-di-dah officers. I came up the hard way. I know what it's like living in a working-class home with a privy at the end of the garden; I know what it's like making ends meet on thirty-five bob a week and queueing up for trams twice a day and having to carry the tin bath into the kitchen of a Saturday night and filling it from the boiler and never having enough hot water so that everyone can have clean; yes, I belonged to that world where you have to go down to the newsagents to make a telephone call, where buying a new suit is a major adventure; where you ruin your few lousy days at Scarborough worrying whether you'll have enough brass to last until you get home; and I too have wondered who the bastards are, in their black coats and pin-stripe trousers, who work out a man's wages so that it's enough, but only just enough, to purchase survival and at the same time screw the last drops of respect and fight out of him.'

Kerr thrust his pipe between his teeth—he reminded Cornish of a pirate clamping his jaws on the blade of a dirk. 'Has Broadbent had any joy with that wireless set of his?'

Cornish told him no.

Kerr shrugged as if the wireless had suddenly become an item of minor importance.

Behind the trenches. Officers and N.C.O.s moved like stage managers fretting away the last moments before curtain.

In the trenches, the men appeared to be treading on the spot as they kept pulling their feet out of the glutinous mud. Their boots were a sorry sight. Designed for use on frosty parade grounds rather than steaming jungles, they were now rotting and disintegrating; comical looking things, some of them, with their soles flapping like idiots' mouths.

Before they left England, the troops had been issued with pith helmets—*sola topis* (the very same ones, it was said, that their grandfathers had worn when they set sail to do battle with the fuzzy-wuzzies, the grandfathers having returned the helmets to Stores after the battle was won). When in the autumn of 1941 the troopship had sailed into Singapore the authorities had shown rare good sense by replacing the quaint headgear with Australian bush hats, infinitely more practical for the jungle.

The British soldiers' principal weapon was known officially as the Short Magazine Lee Enfield Mark III Rifle. It was a venerable weapon that had been issued to the army of King Edward VII, Victoria's son, in 1907. It weighed just over 8½ lb and its pressed steel magazine held 2 clips of 5 215-grain ·303-in. cartridges. The bolt action of the Lee Enfield was claimed by experts to be the fastest in the world. Certainly a thoroughly experienced rifleman could loose as many as 15 rounds at a muzzle velocity of 2,400 feet per second in less than a minute.

But few of the British riflemen on the hill—or indeed anywhere in Malaya—could have been described as thoroughly experienced. Or even experienced. The majority had been in khaki only a matter of months and, for many, embarkation leave had been the first leave of any kind. Officialdom had not of course informed the men of their destination ('Walls Have Ears: The Enemy is Listening') but the more ingenious had devised codes in order to reveal this fact to their families as rapidly as possible. A P.S. to a letter saying 'Love to Auntie Madge' meant that the writer had found himself in North Africa; 'Regards to Uncle John' meant Russia. But for umpteen men the system had broken down. They hadn't included Malaya on the list of likely destinations. Many weren't even sure that they had ever heard of the place.

En route, the troopship had stopped at Capetown. The British soldiers were flabbergasted by the city's beauty and by the hospitality of its citizens. There was little enough time in Capetown—hardly enough time to meet a perfect stranger and become engaged to marry, but half a dozen managed it. Hardly enough time to seduce a girl and leave her pregnant but a few managed it. Hardly enough time to arrange for the sale of five hundred stolen army blankets but one man did. Some soldiers would remember Capetown as a visceral upheaval because their war-shrunken stomachs proved incapable of coping with chocolate and cream buns in gigantic quantities. Some men became incapably drunk and had to be carried back to the ship; others never did return to the ship and thus never completed the journey to Malaya.

Some of the men who did reach Malaya now stood with their feet in mud and stared down the hill at their enemy.

They said little to one another; there seemed to be little to say. Every man had his own thoughts; this was the time to think them.

Cornish walked rapidly. It was unpleasant and uncomfortable in that humidity, but there wasn't much time. Kerr had asked him to 'have a quick look-see before the fun starts.' And soon it would start.

As he walked, Cornish found himself staring intently at familiar sights: the thin bodies of Englishmen protruding from trenches like so many chess-pieces lined up ready for play, the trees angling over them, the great paddle-like leaves, their unreal green. It was as if he was trying to photograph the sights mentally, knowing that in a little while they might never be the same again.

The sun vanished behind dark, ugly clouds.

Cornish concluded his tour. Everyone was on top line. Ready and waiting. But hardly eager.

He made his way along the steep slope above the road. He wondered whether he would die here, for this place. 'David Edward Cornish. R.I.P. He Laid Down His Life For a Place He Had Never Heard Of, In Sector 14F.' No, he didn't. It was a mealy-mouthed euphemism. 'Laying down' suggested some sort of solemn placing on an altar.

Being killed wasn't like that. Not a bit. Being killed was suddenly ceasing to *be*. Finis. The End. Blank screen. End of Performance.

If I get out of this rotten mess, he thought, I shall spend a week in the Savoy—or perhaps even Claridge's—in the company of two, no four, no six beautiful and skilled and deliciously naked courtesans, drinking champagne from solid gold goblets, indulging in every conceivable form of sexual excess, wallowing on a bedspread of breasts and thighs...

No, I won't, he thought. All I'll do is dawdle along Charing Cross Road looking in the bookshops and wishing I had the nerve to wallow on a bedspread of...

He returned to the road.

Morton was sitting on a tree-trunk cleaning his revolver. He was a round, rather cherubic-faced young man of twenty. He began to chat about a Hollywood western he had seen in which Buck Jones fired some fifty shots from his six-gun before pausing to reload.

'Really,' said Cornish. Morton fell silent.

Cornish wiped his face for the umpteenth time. Earlier in the day, Kerr had shown him his massive old Webley ·45, a relic of the Western Front. Kerr said he preferred it to the standard .38-in. revolvers: a Webley had 'grand stopping-power'. It suddenly occurred to Cornish that Kerr must have wanted to be asked about the Webley. About its accuracy and its kick and about the steadiness of the hand needed to tame it. But Cornish hadn't asked; he hadn't any desire to know. He thought of the tiny *kampong* near Kampar. Yet another hasty, disorganized withdrawal. Everyone dashing in every direction. Terror bubbling up in one's gullet like bile. Then the chilling discovery that the enemy was *behind*. The Japs, curse them, had cut the road to the rear. A frantic assembly. Hoarse orders. The late Colonel Brigden led the charge himself. Fix bayonets! Charge! Forward! The battalion thundered down the road like a herd of cattle. Boots sparking on the stones, bayonet blades glinting in the sunlight. Yells. Shouts. Cries. Shots. Men tumbling, their equipment clattering like pots and pans. The colonel had correctly assumed that his rear was threatened not by a major force but only by a light advance detachment. The charge succeeded—no matter that it was away from the enemy's main force. The Japs broke, scattering into the jungle. One of them tripped and fell directly in front of Cornish. There he was, not twenty feet away, trying to scramble to his feet and recover his rifle at the same time. He turned his head as Cornish levelled his revolver. No, he wouldn't surrender. Cornish fired. The bullet hit a leaf a foot from the man's head. Cornish fired again. Missed again. Fired again. Missed again. The Jap rolled from side to side like a man trying desperately to put out a fire in his clothing. Cornish took aim. The Jap had a deep scratch on his face, extending from his left eye to his chin; the top part of the scratch was bleeding but not the lower part. He shielded his face with his elbow but he kept trying to reach his rifle. Kill the sod, Cornish told himself. But someone else did, with a bullet through the right eye from ten feet. The someone was most apologetic. Awfully sorry, he hadn't seen Captain Cornish in all the rush. Cornish told the someone he was jolly lucky he hadn't got himself shot. Afterwards he wondered why he thought he would have more success shooting British troops than Japanese.

'These things are supposed to be accurate up to fifty yards,' said Morton, pointing the revolver at a tree and squinting along the barrel. 'But not in my experience.'

'Nor mine,' said Cornish.

'John Forrester had a funny theory. He said that revolvers

were sexual symbols. He said that constantly cleaning and messing about with one's revolver was tantamount to playing with oneself. Don't you think that's an absolutely absurd theory, sir?'

Cornish said he did indeed.

'At the time,' said Morton, 'I told him that I merely wanted the thing to work properly when needed. I didn't expect it to do much damage but it was awfully comforting to hold. John said that proved his point. An odd chap. I wonder what happened to him.'

'I wonder too,' said Cornish, although he had not once thought of John Forrester since his disappearance outside Serandah.

'Good Lord, I would like a gin and It.,' said Morton.

At that moment the Japanese artillery opened up.

7

It was a crack, a rush of bewildered air, then a roar and an eruption of earth. Beneath Cornish the ground buckled.

A few yards away a man turned and looked up the hill with the inquisitive expression of somebody wondering whether it was a Riley or a Rover that just went whizzing by.

'Take cover!'

Cornish followed his own advice at the moment he shouted. As he hit the ground, a shell burst on the road with an ear-piercing bang. He ducked as a shower of pebbles and dirt cascaded on him. Blast grabbed at him, shoved him, swept past him.

Open-mouthed, he sucked in air.

God.

Where was Morton? He felt the sharp stones digging into his palms as he pushed his weight away from the ground.

God.

Morton's legs and waist were there but the rest of him had vanished. His legs lay stiffly like parts of a dummy. The soles of his boots were badly worn, the left boot more than the right.

Another explosion made Cornish duck away. Again blast ripped at him with hot, angry fingers. This time they'd get him; Christ, this time ...

Trembling, he scrambled to cover behind a log, fresh rope burns still bright on its bark. Poor sod, Morton. But was it

Morton? There was no way to tell. It must have been him; he was sitting there, at that spot. ... What the hell was his first name? John? James? What the hell did it matter now?

A ginger-haired soldier, minus tin hat, emerged to look at Morton's remains. He frowned as if wondering whether it really was Morton.

'It doesn't matter!' Cornish yelled at him.

'Sir?'

Christ. Cornish said, 'Tell Sergeant Hibbs he's in command until relieved. Understand? Quickly, man!'

'Yes, sir, right.'

'And where's your tin hat?'

'What, sir?'

'Never mind. Carry on.'

'Yes, sir.'

The earth shuddered again as a shell walloped into the hill above the road. One of the huts became a whirl of flying bits of *atap*; when the smoke cleared there was nothing but a large hole in the ground and one post wobbling like a drunken man. The shelling had assumed a pattern: four shots in rapid sequence, then a brief pause, followed by one more shot and another pause before the first four were in action again. The air reeked with explosive and burning bamboo.

What I must do, Cornish thought carefully, is get back to H.Q. If H.Q. still exists. I'm not doing any good at all here, cowering behind this silly log.

There was nothing to fight back with, nothing but rifles and Brens. A few 4·5 howitzers were needed. Artillery for the artillery ...

He scrambled to his feet. Now go! he yelled at himself.

He ran along the shoulder of the road, head down, watching the toes of his boots flying over the uneven ground. Hit us again, and again, so that we can once more demonstrate our superb British qualities of dogged endurance and light-hearted lunatic laughter in the face of certain defeat brought upon us by our own stupidity and pig-headedness....

The shells exploded as his feet hit the ground.

He reached the *kampong* and dashed between the huts. The earth sped beneath him. Damned important to tell Kerr of Morton's death, to detach Kirby or Porson or someone to take his place ... to make sure the organization still functioned ...

He heard the shell the same moment it picked him up and turned him over. A wall hit him squarely in the middle of the back. A wall of solid stone, at least three feet thick. He thought what a shame it was that his body was now squashed quite flat; paper-thin, it would flutter and tumble to become a transfer-like decoration on the soil of Malaya. The curious thing was that there was so much time: time to wait in a room with heavy, dark-oak panelling and the smell of varnish: time to study a portrait of Prince Albert: time to listen to a bevy of hirsute gentlemen discussing the building of the Crystal Palace. Then he was watching loose muck and pebbles and dirt, passing, slowing, stopping. Something jarred his shoulder. The left side of his face hurt like hell. A hand flopped before him. He recognized it as his own. Thankfully he saw that it was attached to his arm, which in turn was attached to his shoulder. He tried to take a breath but nothing happened. Did he still possess lungs? Was he dead? No, surely if his shoulder and the left side of his face hurt, he could hardly be dead. And his shoulder and the left side of his face did indeed hurt. Again he tried to take a breath. Again without success. He imagined a gory hole in his chest where his lungs used to be.

Another mind-numbing bang. Hot air took him and flipped him over like the sea flipping over a dead fish on the beach. His arms dropped loosely before him as if they no longer possessed bones. His hands lay with one palm up, one palm down. He observed that the crystal of his watch —'A Little Something with Much Love from Mother and Father, Christmas, 1938'—had cracked.

Dust will get into the works, he thought deliberately.

Suddenly, gloriously, his lungs expanded and he sucked in air. God, it hurt but, God, it was marvellous. He tasted the earth as he gasped for air and still more air.

'He's moving,' he heard a voice say.

'Sir? Are you alive, sir?'

A curious question. Cornish blinked and looked at a minute insect crawling over a pebble.

'Sir?'

'I think 'e's 'ad it.'

'I'm all right,' said Cornish but not loudly enough for anyone to hear. He looked at his legs. They lay in a distressingly ungainly fashion, not unlike Morton's. Would they work? He thought about it for a moment then, timorously, he attempted to move a foot.

'He's alive! Get 'im!'

Fingers clutched at his shoulders. There was a moment of confused tumbling and slithering, an unpleasant dig in the kidneys from something that felt like a boot, a curse from someone with a Cockney accent.

Milne's apologetic voice:

'Awfully sorry, old man. We dropped you.'

Cornish wiped muck from his eyes. He saw Tom Byrne's face beside Milne's.

'I'm all right,' he said. 'I'm not dying. I don't need the last bloody rites.'

'I wouldn't dream of giving them to you,' beamed Tom.

'I was jolly relieved to see you move,' said Milne.

Only your jaw was relieved, Cornish thought dully. He looked about him. Boots. Legs. He was on the muddy bottom of a trench.

'Nothing broken?' Tom enquired.

'I don't think so. I'm going to get up in a minute, when I've caught my breath. We'll know then, I suppose.'

'I think he was just winded,' said Milne. He stood up and peered cautiously over the lip of the trench. 'Accurate, eh, their artillery?'

As if on cue, a shell wooshed overhead and the hill shuddered anew. A light shower of dirt descended on the trench, pattering audibly on steel helmets.

Tom Byrne crouched in the trench. 'Your face seems a bit of a mess,' he said to Cornish.

'You should see Morton's face.'

'Morton's?'

'Never mind.' Cornish felt sick and dizzy. He tried to wipe the confusion from his eyes. He said to Milne, 'Morton's dead. We'll have to put someone in his place. Porson, I suppose.'

Milne frowned. 'Porson? Do you think so?'

Cornish sighed. 'We don't have much choice, do we?'

'No, I suppose not. All right. I'll get word to him.'

'Have you seen Major Kerr?'

'Not since the shooting started.'

Even as he spoke, delivering himself of sounds of logic and duty, panic took hold. He could feel it, the old enemy; he could observe its progress as it sped through him, from nerve to nerve, muscle to muscle, like some foul ailment. His hand thrust into the soft mud of the trench floor. His legs curled beneath him. I must not let go, he said to himself as deliberately as he was able ... not here, not in front of everyone ... it wouldn't do ... it would be a terribly bad show....

Then, quite suddenly, he found himself moderately calm again.

A shell burst with a stunning din; the trench wall sagged and strained.

'Rather close, what?' Milne grinned. 'Are you all right, old man?'

'Of course,' said Cornish. 'Why not?'

Cornish found his cap. It was caked with mud and one corner was torn, revealing the oilskin lining. Where the hell, he wondered, did I leave my tin hat?

'I've got to push off,' he told Milne. He had to find Kerr.

Tom Byrne said, 'God be with you.'

Cornish looked at him. '*With* me? He can go *instead* of me!'

He started to giggle; it was a hell of a funny remark. But poor old Tom was looking away, disappointed, like a magician whose trick has gone awry.

8

Private Ernest George Kerr saw his first enemy projectile in 1915. It was a German canister shell and it came wobbling at him out of a bright winter sun. A harmless-looking thing, rather like an oil drum. It hurtled over his head and exploded on the trench well above and behind him—and discharged a far from harmless swath of scrap: bent and corroded nails, bits of ancient farm implements, chunks of shrapnel, shapeless remains of bullets, broken rifle barrels, pieces of iron, fragments of glass. A rusty chisel blade hit the man standing next to Kerr—his name was Hardcastle and he hailed from Kitton Priors, Shropshire—and neatly removed most of the left side of his head.

That evening Private Kerr had joined the queue outside the Red Lamp, a ten-franc note clutched firmly in a damp hand, a smear of Hardcastle's brains still dark on his sleeve. He had decided. Bugger the chances of catching a dose—the chances were a damn sight better that he'd be blown to bits long before Peter started to itch. And bugger saving himself for some nice lass—Gladys Pertwee, for example—likely as not there'd be nowt to save. Time was short. If he was going to find out about wick-dipping, he'd better get on with it. It was now or, in all probability, never. Every few minutes the men shuffled forward a few feet. A man said, 'They've got two of 'em on tonight. It's better when there's three, but 'orrible when there's only the one.' After an hour and twenty-six minutes, Kerr parted with his ten-franc note and watched it vanish into a pink and white jar adroitly placed

59

at arm's length from the dead centre of the bed. But no smile accompanied the payment of the fee. No welcome sparkled in the grey-brown eyes. A hasty puff from a Gauloise; a yawn. A shrug in reply to his mumbled words. A scratching of the head in preparation for the next tedious round. Curiously, the Frenchwoman's attitude failed utterly to dampen Kerr's enthusiasm. Indeed, he was only dimly aware of the woodenness of her features and the thickness and gracelessness of her body. The details of her didn't really matter. What did matter was the fact that a naked female—a naked, *willing* female—lay on a bed waiting for him. At last! As he doffed his tunic and slipped the H.M. Government-issue braces from his shoulders and undid the sharp, pressed steel buttons of his fly, the last remnants of his nervousness vanished. This was bloody bully, this was! Down came his trousers, off came his boots. Right, Peter, old lad, this is what you've been waiting for ... no more just *thinking* about it, wondering what it's like ... it's there, ripe and ready!

Mary Pickford.

He closed his eyes as, with businesslike fingers, the woman guided him to his goal. And suddenly there was no taint of garlic and weary sweat, no draughty hut, no scraping of cold, impatient boots outside—only Mary Pickford, fresh from her perfumed bath, squirming prettily beside him on a feathered bed, ecstatic with the way his stomach was polishing hers, supremely delighted with her seduction by Private Ernest George Kerr..

The seconds fled—one hundred and two of them. Then it was Guy Fawkes night, the firing of the cannons at the Tattoo, the gusting-by of the London-to-Edinburgh.

Sweet peace.

But not for long. The Gauloise had burned only a centimetre or two; once more it was gripped by thin, passionless lips. Time was up, soldier boy; others waited; he was to take his things and get dressed in the *toilette,* the door on the right....

Kerr didn't sleep that night. His being palpitated with thoughts of women. Their bodies, slim, plump, brown, yellow, white, slithered past him in sensuous procession, breasts bouncing in merry time, a wondrous array of mounds of fatty areolar tissue and lactiferous ducts ... bellies soft and warm and downy ... hands gentle and probing and utterly without shame. God, there were countless bloody *millions* of women! All of them different, yet all of them mounting the same marvellous equipment, all with tits to touch and knickers to pull down.

With passionate sincerity he prayed that he might be spared on the field of battle. Surely God could see that it would be a *crime* to let him die now ... now that he had just found out what it was all about.

And next time, he swore, he wouldn't go charging in like a bull in the Co-op; next time he would make it last a bit, get his money's worth.

He assured God that he really didn't care particularly about surviving to a ripe old age; it was only the next few, urgent years that concerned him.

What a feeling! A woman's bare legs on either side of yours and her tits squashed under you like two nicely filled hot-water bottles.

When Corporal Kerr (his stripes came through two days after his introduction to German canister shells and French prostitutes) went on his first leave to Rochdale, he was, incredibly, unwounded and undiseased. He had had sex seventy-eight times, with twelve different women, all French, all whores. (He was keeping a rough mental tally.) Now he was able to enjoy them—no matter how impatient they became—for as much as eight minutes at a time. He had on occasion paid an additional five francs for certain variations on the theme. There was so much to learn. Sex was like an enormous continent that had suddenly been opened to him, the tireless explorer. It struck him what an appalling tragedy it was that so many people stayed at home, so to speak. Corporal Evans, for example, a dour old man of forty, went to the whores regularly but with no more enthusiasm than he displayed going to the latrines. On the other hand, a wide-eyed Liverpudlian named Winfield never went to the whores at all. He claimed that they were instruments of the devil and that consorting with them was to guarantee endless agony in Perdition. Sourby, a married man, invariably returned from the Red Lamp bitter with detestation of himself and his vile lusts. Indeed, none of Kerr's comrades seemed to share his unmitigated enthusiasm for sex; none talked of the subject with other than giggles or the deepest gloom. For some time the fact troubled Kerr; eventually, however, he realized quite positively that he was right and they were unquestionably wrong.

Since enlisting he had corresponded with a Miss Gladys Pertwee who lived at 14 Lucknow Lane, Rochdale. In both the Kerr and the Pertwee homes it was *understood* that 'our Ernie' would eventually, God willing, wed 'our Gladys'. She was a strapping young woman with rosy cheeks and a merry smile; she worked at Jas. P. Heslop & Son, Dispensing Chemist.

On his first day home, after a high tea of cowheel pie (his favourite dish), Kerr put on his cap and strode along to Drake Street to the establishment of Jas. P. Heslop & Son. It was five minutes to closing time. A glorious evening, warm and dry. He felt lightheaded with happiness. When he opened the shop door, it played something right delectable on its brass bell. Gladys, her sweet face alive with joy, beamed at him over the shoulder of a man who wanted something for his hæmorrhoids. By God, but she was a grand lass! He ached to hold her; instead, a-tremble, he grinned at a display card advertising Pear's soap. He heard Gladys telling the man how to apply the stuff and thanking him for his patronage and wishing him a very good evening indeed. A flower, no less! A blossom! Somehow, in those glowing moments, Gladys became the reason all the armies of Europe were tearing at each other's throats. She was the prize. And he had won her.

He thought.

At midnight, Kerr returned home, heavy with the weight of still-shackled lust. He washed his face. He felt sick. What an evening! Hour after hour of it—and all he got was a bit of a touch of her right tit and not even the nipple, at that! Who in his right mind would have guessed? ... Never once did it cross his mind that she might refuse, not once, in all those feverish hours of thinking about her and imagining what she would feel like.... And to think he hadn't gone to the Red Lamp, not once, for a *month* before his leave.

She had said no. Over and over again. Oh yes, she loved him, she said, and if he really loved her he wouldn't try to do it. Even for properly engaged couples it wasn't right. A girl should go to her marriage bed unsullied.

Unsullied? He wasn't sure what the word meant but he had a depressingly good idea.

The weather was fine. The evenings continued warm and dry. But Gladys was unyielding. Beast! she called him. What sort of a lass did he think she was? It was a question he thought it best not to answer. On the third evening, she permitted him a brief handling of her right breast, though not her left. On the fourth evening both breasts were won. Plump and sweet. Kerr kissed them. Gladys giggled. But when he tried to direct her hand she clenched it and hit him quite savagely with it. On the fifth evening, they talked little, walking in sullen silence until half past nine. Then, a tiny, shy smile. A touching of hands. All forgiven. Bliss. Kisses and clutching. Down on the gentle turf. She was deliciously pliant. She whimpered as he kissed her and touched her. This time, surely, victory was his! His hands slipped and strained between her hooks and buttons and, at last, still bearing the pattern of good Bradford cotton, her breasts came free. Now there could be no stopping him! A rubbery nipple in his mouth, he sent his right hand off exploring.

It was resoundingly slapped.

No; he was to go no further! She was adamant.

'Good God,' he said, genuinely astonished.

'I don't know what you've learnt in France, Ernie Kerr, but you want to remember, this is Rochdale!'

'And you can bloody well keep it!' said Kerr, springing to his feet and striding away, leaving her with her virginity unsullied.

The next evening Kerr drank half a dozen pints of watery wartime bitter with a pimply, flat-footed school chum named Humphrey who was getting eleven pounds a week in a munitions factory plus (he confided) 'all the you-know-what I need from the soldiers' wives on the line, poor lonely dears.' To complete the evening, the Hull train brought Uncle Derwent who devoted two hours to a detailed explanation of his master plan for beating the Boche once and for all.

On the final evening of his leave, the door knocker clattered at precisely twenty-two minutes past six. It was Gladys. She said she had thought it over and she would.

He stared at her. She still wore her bonnet and she was pink of cheek from walking all the way from Jas. P. Heslop & Son.

'You what?' he said.
'You know what I mean,' she said.
'Well, I ...'
'Don't you want it now?'
'Oh ... aye ...'
'Well then, you can have it.'
'I can?'
'Aye, you can.'
But her jaw was so firmly set, and although it was as pretty a jaw as ever, it seemed to say Tactical Reverse rather than Sweet Surrender.
'Er, when?' he enquired.
'Well, you're going back tomorrow so it had better be tonight, hadn't it?' she said, frostily logical.
'All right then ... where?'
'I don't mind.'
'We could ... go for a stroll ...'
'All right,' she said. Bravely.

The next morning, Kerr caught the train south. He sat on his kit bag in the packed corridor, his rifle between his knees, and gazed at Lancashire speeding by. He didn't see it. No matter how he tried, no matter how he filled his mind with such stimulating tasks as naming Queen Victoria's nine children or King George V's five, or mentally field-stripping and re-assembling the Lee Enfield rifle component by component, or even cataloguing the battles in which the regiment had won battle honours, he kept seeing Gladys. And she was flat out on the grass, reaching matter-of-factly into her clothes and undoing them, lifting her breasts out of her bodice like superb fruits from a bowl and lying back with her features in the same mask of patient martyrdom that Joan of Arc must have worn on her way to the stake. At the time he believed that he had Achieved Success. Here at last was the prize that went only to the brave. But as he panted and strained over her unresisting but totally unco-operative form, the realization struck him hard—this was no prize at all; this was a sacrifice! It chilled him, finished him. As he walked home, he wondered glumly how man had ever raped if it wasn't desired by the female.

Thank God for the Red Lamp.

You knew where you stood with those bints.

Kerr capped his fountain pen. The crack of the first Japanese shells had set off the train of thought. The memories had pounded along like a film run much too rapidly. Pretty Gladys Pertwee. She had been issued with all the right equipment but she hadn't a clue how to use it. What was worse, she thought herself so bloody lovely that she hadn't to bother learning. One could forgive the first but, unless one was completely daft, not the second.

He closed his notebook and pocketed it. The report would have to wait—which was a pity because he was just warming to the task of stating the facts of the deaths of the senior officers and how he, E. G. Kerr, Major, had taken over and had prepared the positions in anticipation of immediate attack by the enemy. The disposition of the troops, the locations of the mines, the tank trap, the logs ... it all made a neat, logical story, one that, God knows, might be studied by historians and junior officers in years to come ...

Don't be daft, he said to himself.

McGregor, pale and tiny, was hovering around the hut entrance, wincing as the shells boomed.

'Have you seen Captain Cornish?'

'No sir, I haven't, sir.'

'See if you can find him, will you?'

'I'll do that, sir.'

He scurried away down the hill.

Kerr strode after him. No point in staying in the hut. It would probably be blown to bits in a little while. No matter; McGregor had said that he had found a cave and he was fixing it up, soon he would have it ready. Funny little bugger, McGregor; he would make someone a grand wife one of these days.

As he walked, Kerr wondered briefly about Gladys Pertwee. What had happened to her? Was she married? A grandmother by now? Then he forgot about her and never again thought of her.

Behind Kerr the first shells hit the top of the hill, framing the huts with black mushrooms of dirt and smoke.

A platoon of Japanese troops could be seen, hurrying along the road at the foot of the hill. They vanished; it looked as if the jungle had eaten them.

The Japs were shooting well. You had to hand it to them. Very neat grouping of rounds. Wallop one sector good and proper, then move on to the next. A thoroughly professional effort, though hardly intense by Flanders standards.

A chunk of tree went whirring into the air like a propeller. It spun back to earth and shattered. A hut burned furiously. Kerr ducked as the air above him writhed, protesting the passage of a shell which exploded on the hill fifty yards away. He straightened his cap. Shells were the same the world over: after a time you got to know whether they were going to fall short of you or beyond you. Or on you. Kerr dusted his shoulder. Another thing you could rely on was dirt.

Somebody was yelling for help.

For some reason Kerr thought of his father: the wasted, grey-skinned face with its much-too-bright eyes, a mockery of life on harsh white hospital sheets. Kerr hoped his father knew of this day and the fact that his son was commanding a battalion of the British Army.

A bit of pride is good for a man, he thought; perhaps even after he's dead.

It was easy to spot the artillery locations. Little dots of flame sparkled in the foliage and leaves and branches kept jumping about as though stung.

If only we had ... He stopped himself; it was pointless to waste time thinking about using equipment he didn't possess and couldn't possibly obtain.

A couple of orderlies scurried across the road. But the yelling for help continued.

Kerr looked along the line of men huddled like moles in their trenches. Artillery shook them rigid; they hadn't yet learnt how much respect to accord it. They still had to find out that artillery makes a hell of a lot of noise and smoke and digs holes and knocks down trees and buildings with spectacular gusto, but in spite of all that, artillery is an inefficient means of killing dug-in troops.

I suppose, he thought, it's up to me to teach them.

He tugged down the skirt of his jacket and glanced at it to make sure no dirt was clinging to it. A deep breath. All right, my lad, he said to himself, let's be getting on with it.

He jogged down the steep slope to the road. The loose gravel skittered beneath his boots; for one awful instant he thought he was going to slip and fall. Sweat sprang from startled pores. Oops. Balance regained. Thank Christ.

Across the road half a dozen Tommies stared at him over the lip of their trench.

He wished them a very good afternoon. How were they settling in? He trusted the Nips weren't inconveniencing them too much.

For a moment the men were hesitant, unsure how to answer him. Then they allowed themselves to be persuaded that they weren't scared half out of their wits, that things weren't really too unpleasant, that the Japanese bombardment was a minor irritation, nothing more.

Grand.

Kerr strode on to the next trench, his boots crunching purposefully on the loose stones, his swagger-stick beating a brisk tattoo on his thigh. He felt intensely alive—as he always did in times of extreme danger. The greater the likelihood of imminent death or injury the keener the content of the moment. In November 1940 he had spent a night with a Mrs Martin Cooper-Yeadon whose husband was away commanding a destroyer or frigate or something (she wasn't sure which). The Germans were also active that night. Bombs kept tumbling out of the sky to burst in terrifying proximity to the hotel in which Kerr and Mrs Cooper-Yeadon were staying. Death seemed only moments away. At one point the hotel apparently moved several yards down the Strand towards Nelson's Column. Walls sagged and cracked; ceilings spewed plaster; pictures tumbled. But in Room 24 Kerr and Mrs Cooper-Yeadon remained inosculated. Indeed, each explosion outside engendered fresh fervour inside. The next morning, in the cool brightness of the breakfast-room, both agreed that danger had added the last delicious ingredient; it had been a truly magnificent night's manoeuvres.

Wide eyes stared at him from beneath steel helmet-rims. The lads thought he was mad, walking about. In a little while, though, they would agree that it wasn't madness at all but a complete and utter contempt for the enemy.

Cornish was pulling himself out of a trench. He looked pale and shaken up. His face was scratched and bleeding.

'Hullo, Dave. What happened?'

Cornish looked up at him. His mouth was slightly open. He seemed to be asking himself whether this nit of a major had noticed that the enemy was shelling the place.

'Sir ... look out, sir.'

69

'You seem to have hurt your face a bit.'
'What? Oh, it's nothing.'
'Better let the M.O. have a look.'
'I will, sir, but ...'

It was grand for the id, chatting this way, with half a hundred pairs of pop-eyes on you. Of course it would all be spoiled if a shell landed ten yards away and blew you arse over breakfast. But the chances were bloody good that it wouldn't. And it was a chance worth taking. Kerr scratched the tip of his nose. He told Cornish that he was going to have a look around. Would Cornish care to come?

9

The madman walked erect.
Like a squire taking a turn around his estate, Kerr strolled, tap-tap-tapping away with his swagger-stick. Cornish watched him. What the hell was he trying to prove? That the Jap shells didn't frighten him? If so, he was a moron, because only a moron could fail to be scared bloody stiff of the Jap shells.
One landed beside the burning hut, close to the spot where the colonel and the two majors had been buried. Cornish grimaced, thinking of their bodies being uprooted. Then he wondered why he thought it worse to blow corpses to pieces than living men.
A piece of *atap* came fluttering down like a wounded bird.
Kerr now stopped and stood at the roadside, chatting with the troops, telling them that he thought they would have had a saloon bar fixed up in their trench by now.
The men liked that. Even in the middle of a bombardment, men warmed to the notion of their being rogues.
'We can manage a cup of cocoa, sir.'
'Love one,' said Kerr. It sounded like 'loov'. 'And one for Captain Cornish here, if you please.'
Cornish started to say he didn't want one—but Kerr would probably take it as an insult to the men's cocoa-making ability or something equally asinine.
The earth shuddered. Cornish ducked instinctively. But

Kerr, the mad bastard, didn't even blink. As if deaf to the high-explosive din, he continued to sip his cocoa while flattering the men's poor egos with fictions about their prowess with women and alcohol. His eyes heavy with mock sadness, he described a group of riflemen as 'a bad lot of buggers' and they grinned in delight. He told a scrawny, ill-nourished product of industrial twentieth-century Britain that his escapades in Singapore were scandalous and that the authorities were at this very moment trying to establish precisely how many of the colony's maidens he had deflowered. Watery eyes sparkled; thin cheeks reddened. It was, Cornish told himself as he listened, allegiance being exchanged for outrageous bullshit. But it was also, he frankly admitted, a transaction quite beyond his own powers. Men's hearts didn't warm to a voice that was too cold, too correct; they weren't captivated by a manner distant and introverted. Don't you try to be a personality, he told himself; it really wouldn't suit you.

A lance-corporal had been hit by shrapnel and was bleeding profusely from a wound in his side.

'Hold on, lad. You'll be all right. Nowt to worry about.'

The voice was gentle, fatherly. Kerr sat by the man and held his shoulder and talked to him until the orderlies arrived. Then he was in another trench and the riflemen were swarming about him in the almost mechanical way of creatures who desperately need confidence and leadership. As he beamed at the men, Kerr stood upright, his head and shoulders totally exposed above the lip of the trench. It can only be a matter of time, Cornish told him silently, before you get your silly head blown off.

He had to declare it to himself as a statement of fact. He had to remind himself that what Kerr was doing was outside the bounds of rational behaviour. It was idiotic not to duck, not to try to avoid being killed. It made no sense.

But neither does war, Cornish thought. Perhaps, therefore, senseless behaviour makes the most sense in warfare. Is Kerr incredibly brave or incredibly stupid? Or both?

The barrage ended suddenly.

The jungle was utterly silent. Every creature seemed to be holding its breath. Even the air was still.

Then, after a few moments, there was a rustling, a squawking. The jungle resumed its frenetic activity as if the artillery barrage had never taken place.

On the hill the British troops readied themselves. Johnny Jap was on his way now; soon he would be in view. Magazines and bolts were checked yet again. Men narrowed their eyes as they stared. Unconsciously they scraped with nervous fingernails on their own hands; some drew blood without noticing.

'Any time now,' said Kerr. He looked around at the sky as if fearing that the weather might stop play.

Cornish was aware of the sweaty, funky smell of himself. Wryly he thought of advertisements that the agency had created telling of the social dangers of body odour.

Kerr charged his pipe and turned his back on the enemy to light it. He sucked the smoke with relish. 'Tobacco's getting low. Only enough for two or three smokes, then I'll give it up. I've been meaning to for years. It's not good for one, you know.'

Cornish nodded automatically. He had given up smoking. Once. It was a hell of a battle. Weeks of craving, of dreaming about cigarettes and cigars. Then, entire sequences of three and four minutes at a time in which tobacco wasn't the only subject in his mind. The battle had almost been won when he had accepted a Craven 'A' at a party to celebrate the awarding of the Harry Hill Holiday Camp account to Cornish-McIlraith.

73

'Funny, him not attacking the moment the artillery shut up.'

'Very funny.'

Kerr smiled. He peered down at the jungle. Then he shook his head. 'No good,' he said, 'I'll have to wear the bloody things.' He produced his glasses and breathed noisily on the lenses. 'It's distances that bother me. I can still read the newspaper; not a bit of trouble. Even the telephone book. But I'm buggered when it comes to distances. Time bloody well marches on.'

The wind flickered through the tall trees, the 150-foot-high giants that towered over the jungle. An animal, a monkey or something similar, jumped from one tree to the next and scurried away into the foliage.

Kerr stiffened. He nudged Cornish. 'There, Dave, see? Down there by the road.'

Yes, there they were. Lined up, in neat ranks. Rifles at identical angles. Japanese Infantrymen: At Attention: Sixpence Each or Five Shillings the Set of Twelve....

Clips of cartridges were pushed down on the magazine springs; bolts thudded home, thrusting ·303-inch brass cartridges into the breech. The Bren-gun crews clipped their pans of ammunition (36 rounds per pan) in place and swung their weapons on the tripod mounts; then they sat back because they had been ordered to hold their fire until otherwise instructed.

Kerr gazed at the line of troops, his head slowly turning from left to right. He nodded, his great jaw thrust forward; he seemed to approve.

Cornish wondered inconsequentially whether Kerr was pleased with them or with himself for having created them.

The reports from the west, east and south were negative.

'He's going to come straight up the hill,' said Kerr. 'He wants to find out how serious we are. He will that!'

Sweat formed in tiny globules along his upper lip. He took off his cap and wiped his forehead with his arm but he didn't touch the sweat on his lip.

'Must be a funny business, advertising,' he said unexpectedly.

'Not particularly,' said Cornish.

'Lot of brass in it, though.'

'It depends.'

'Depends?'

'On whether you have clients who spend lots on advertising. What you make depends entirely on how much space your client buys.'

'Space?'

'Pages in magazines, or posters in the streets.'

'Ah, I see. Very interesting.' He chuckled delightedly. 'My, but this is a grand position. We could hold it for ever! We've lots of ammo and food and water. And after a bit the air force will come and drop more supplies. There's no telling how long we can hold on here.'

Cornish said flatly, 'And when the time comes I suppose the air force can drop our old-age pension cheques to us as well.'

Kerr sniffed, half amused. Then: 'Christ, look!'

The Japanese began to move.

Through the shadows of the jungle they came, the metal of their weapons glinting dully.

'Hold your fire till ordered,' someone said. A man coughed.

Kerr took his ancient Webley from its holster and spun the cylinder to check that it was working smoothly.

For all the world the Japanese troops looked like sturdy little mountaineers as they took the slope. From where the British riflemen watched and waited, the attackers' legs seemed too short for their bodies. They were shrimps, short-arses. But dangerous. No one kidded himself that they weren't.

The Japanese were confined by the terrain. Some walked on the road itself, some on either side of it. They held their 7-lb. 12-oz. Model-99 rifles with the easy balance of men inured to such burdens.

'No firing until you get the word. Is that understood?'

The section leaders paced behind their charges, fearful that one of them might disgrace himself by pulling his trigger too soon.

Cornish wanted to relieve himself. He turned. McGregor was in the first Bedford's driver's seat, as arranged.

It should work, Cornish thought. It really should.

'I remember there was a captain at Loos,' said Kerr. 'I admired him because he never raised his voice. Didn't matter what the hell was going on around him, he always talked normally. Said it calmed the men. I think he was right. But I can never remember to do it. I always bellow!' He thrust his pipe between his teeth. 'I wish we'd thought to pick up some barbed wire from somewhere. It would have come in very handy now, wouldn't it?'

'Very,' said Cornish. He cleared his throat because the word emerged as a squeak.

The sun slid from behind a cloud like a spotlight for the main act. The Japanese were bent forward, walking more cautiously now, lowering their heads. One of their officers, a slim man with glasses and a moustache, wearing an open-necked shirt, snapped something at the men around him; he gesticulated with his pistol. It looked as if he was telling them to close up or open up or, perhaps, hurry up. The men looked at him and nodded with quick little motions but they seemed to continue their trudging as before.

'Just about now, I think,' said Kerr.

Cornish raised his hand behind him.

The Japs' boots could be heard crunching on the loose stones of the road. Cornish's eyes flicked from feet to faces. Skinny cheeks: square jaw: the unlucky one. Cornish dropped his hand, signalling McGregor to turn the ignition key in the Bedford.

The explosion sounded curiously tinny. Cornish could spare only a fleeting glance at the smoke and the flying dirt and the skinny man toppling sideways, his rifle spinning from his outstretched arm. He turned to the man in the second Bedford; his hand dropped again. As the second mine exploded, the riflemen opened fire. At once half a dozen Japanese fell, slumping as if boneless. Bolts clattered as sweating hands yanked them up and back and forward and down. A Japanese officer was hit in the thigh; he managed to stagger a few yards, barely able to maintain his balance; he clutched at his wound and his mouth dropped open. A second bullet caught him in the chest and he went over backwards. Near him, a man lay on his back staring at the sun, his left arm striking the ground again and again.

Now the Japanese sought any cover they could find. They returned the British fire steadily, like the well-trained soldiers they were, balancing their Model-99s on the palms of their left hands, working bolts and triggers with their right hands. Empty cartridge cases sparkled as they tumbled from smoking breeches.

One Japanese infantryman attempted to rally his comrades by charging the British positions. Yelling something, he tried to run, but his attempt was ludicrous. He slipped on the steep incline just as the British riflemen had slipped on it during the night. He fell. Clumsily, awkwardly. He tried to get up but two bullets caught him almost at the same instant. The shocking impact tipped him over backwards as if he had been kicked. Gracelessly he tumbled, a flurry of arms and legs. His rifle and helmet went slithering after him.

The British had all the advantages. All the cover. And, now, all the confidence.

'Well done, lads! That's the spirit! That's the way it's done!' Kerr looked like a vicar smiling upon his flock at a church picnic. Everyone, it seemed, was behaving in an exemplary manner.

Cornish watched the Japanese as they withdrew. They backed down the hill, clutching their rifles at waist level and pumping round after round at the British positions. One Jap was hit in the chest. He dropped his rifle and sat down abruptly. He looked as if he was contemplating, for he cupped his chin in one hand and rocked slowly backwards and forwards. Then he rolled over and lay still. Further up the slope a fallen Jap beat the ground with his fist, apparently in impotent anger at the cruel fortune of war. Did he feel disgraced because he had been wounded and therefore could not continue to do battle for the glory of the Emperor? Cornish wondered whether the poor devil would consider a bullet in the head as a favour.

The shooting became spasmodic. It ceased.

'Bloody good show!' beamed Kerr. He stood up and bellowed along the line of dug-in riflemen. 'I warned them! I told them not to try! But they wouldn't listen!'

Cornish smiled; it was hard not to. Kerr had a way of putting over a half-decent line. And his ebullience was infectious. Cornish felt in his pocket for a cigarette. Kerr is happy because the Japs are retreating, Cornish thought wryly, and I'm glum because I know damn well that they will soon attack again.

Kerr said, 'They were just probing that time. They wanted to know how serious we are. It was worth a few buggers' lives. They'll be back.'

'And I don't think it will be long,' said Cornish.
'That's what the actress said to the bishop!' chortled Kerr with a hoot of a laugh. He folded his glasses and put them back in their imitation crocodile-hide case.

10

The shelling had cost the British three men dead and two wounded, one seriously. The infantry assault, however, had failed to scratch even one man. But the Japanese had left more than twenty dead on the hill, little bundles of cheap cotton and waxy flesh. A rifle stood as a monument to the brief action, its bayonet buried to the hilt, its stock wobbling heavily in the wind.

After a meal of corned beef and tea, the British troops buried their dead. Tom Byrne said the appropriate words and the bodies—or what was left of them after treatment by high explosive—were lowered into the ground wrapped in blankets.

The trenches were deepened. Bits of bamboo matting were found and used as duckboards. Empty ammunition boxes filled with dirt formed a useful parapet along the tops of the trenches. Men worked hard on their bits of trenches; they felt proprietary about them now that they had successfully denied them to the enemy.

'It's still the same,' said Broadbent. 'I think I'm transmittin' but nothin's comin' in.'

Cornish nodded. He told Broadbent to keep trying. Damn the bloody wireless set! Why the hell couldn't it work properly?

What a stupid question, he thought.

For the moment there was nothing to do. Except wait for the next assault. No more organizing to do; no more ammo to unload and conceal; no more field telephones to site; no more men to order and allot. It had all been done. With moderate efficiency.

Kerr was asleep. Sensible old soldier, he slept whenever circumstances permitted.

Cornish sat down and re-read the last letter he had received from home. His mother wrote of shows and relatives; his father wrote of happenings at the agency. Both of them undoubtedly believed that the subjects would bring home nearer to him for a few minutes. Oddly enough, they had quite the opposite effect; they were too remote; they belonged to another world, another time. One simply couldn't relate.

Tom Byrne came striding along.

'The rest of the chaps have asked me to make a formal request,' said Cornish. 'We would very much like a miracle, please.'

Tom grinned. 'What do you have in mind?'

'We were thinking of having the jungle open up and swallow the Japs. Do you think we could have that one?'

'No harm in asking, I guess.'

Cornish scratched his head. 'Hell, Tom, I wish you'd gone with the runners. Now it's too bloody late. You are a stubborn sod.'

'It's your company, David. I can't tear myself away!'

Cornish suddenly asked Tom Byrne why he had decided to become a priest. Then he apologized for asking. He wasn't sure why he had. Perhaps it was simply that he found it remarkably easy to communicate with Tom. He felt no reserve, no awkwardness.

'I'm flattered that you're interested,' Tom said. 'But let me ask you something. Do you think being a priest is worthwhile?'

'God knows ... Sorry; that was unintentional. I don't

know much about it but it all seems rather narrow to me. There's so much to see, to experience....'

'If I told you that serving God and one's fellow man is the most rewarding work in the world, I guess you wouldn't believe me.'

'I'd think you had told yourself that so many times that you were finally convinced.'

'OK, in that case I won't tell you.'

'What part of America are you from?'

'A town called Lackawanna, near Buffalo, upper New York State. How about you?'

'London. Near Wimbledon. In southern England.'

'I've heard of it.'

'What's Lackawanna like?'

'Kind of dirty. Industrial plants. And too much snow in the wintertime. My, but I hated the stuff. When I was a kid I seemed to spend all winter shovelling snow from the porch and the path. Now I miss it more than anything, I think. I can't tell you how much I'd love to make a snowball, feel that crisp snow burning my fingers—then pitch it and see it go down some guy's neck!'

'Some Protestant guy's neck, no doubt.'

'Indubitably, old boy,' smiled Tom, trying with limited success to sound like an upper-crust Britisher.

Cornish broke a cigarette and handed half to Tom. 'No hard feelings in spite of your callous religious persecution.'

'Thanks, David. That's generous of you.'

'No, I'm just trying to make sure of a place up there.'

Cornish dragged the smoke into his lungs. It savoured of Regent Street and lunch at Pimm's and the smell of new car leather.

Tom puffed the Player's with a delight that, Cornish thought, could only be described as unholy. An entirely likeable human being, Tom. Cornish watched him for a

82

few moments. Then he said, 'Are you scared, Tom?'
'Of what? Dying?'
'Yes. Or having half your face blown off. Or your stomach spread over a couple of acres. We have an unexcelled selection of things to be scared of.'
Tom nodded. 'Sometimes I'm scared,' he said. 'It means of course that my faith is being tested. *I* am being tested. At such times I try to tell myself that it's foolish to be frightened because nothing can possibly happen to me in this world that will make any real difference. Sure, it can hurt me; it can even kill me. But that's not important, not in the long run.'
'I see.'
'I haven't convinced you.'
'I suppose I'm more interested in the short run,' said Cornish. He smiled and took a long drag of his cigarette, pulling on it until it began to burn his lips. Tom Byrne had the Bible; Kerr had King's Regs. All one needed was the right book.

The troops watched Cornish in silence from their dugouts. Their heads turned to him as he walked by. A succession of heads each bearing a face: thin, fat, ugly, attractive, vacant, intelligent, crafty, ingenuous ... Mass produced faces. Fifty-Shilling-Suit faces. Other ranks' faces. A Major Somebody-or-Other, Scotch and soda in porky hand, had, without warning, declared how few men with *individual* faces emerged from the ranks. And, he said, all one needed to do in order to verify the fact was to look at them—but at the *faces*, not at the buttons and boots. 'They come out of perhaps a dozen moulds,' said the major, 'and within those groupings the sods are practically indistinguishable.' In his opinion, a generation or two of *some* sort of means was essential to the creation of features of distinction. 'Call me snobbish if you like,' he had said—and, oddly enough, no one had, 'but do you ever see any of those other ranks' faces in boardrooms or clubs?' Hateful. Yet there seemed to be a cruel morsel of truth in there somewhere. Did Major Somebody-or-Other have a face of distinction? Cornish couldn't remember. He wondered what he would look like if his father had been a chimney sweep.

Towards evening the Japanese attacked again.

They waved swords and blew whistles and shouted what were presumably war cries and surged up the open slope. Their bayonets sparkled in the late afternoon sun; their teeth glittered as their mouths opened to suck in the hot air. Crouched, determined, they advanced, their eyes fixed on the British line.

As they came nearer you could almost hear them panting.

The last sticks of dynamite were exploded. A man's leg suddenly angled inwards from the knee; he fell stiffly, awkwardly, and he looked at his shattered leg with astonished eyes. Another man was blown to pieces by an explosion. Fourteen pieces.

At once the rifle fire burst from the defenders. A wave of bullets slammed into the leading infantry. Some bullets passed right through men, slicing a clean path through muscle and flesh and slowing by only about one-third in velocity. Other bullets struck bone and curled into cruel shapes despite the layer of cupro-nickel applied to the surface of each round as required by the Geneva Convention.

The Japs were brave—you had to give them that. Their courage was awesome. They had been told to get to the top of the hill and kick the British off. That was precisely what they intended to do.

Only one way to stop them: kill them. Shoot them down as fast as they come. Knock 'em off, one by one. Jam in clip after clip. Squeeze trigger. Bolt up, back, forward, down. Rifle gets hotter than hell. No time to worry about it. Keep shooting. Line up target with foresight and notch. Aim for the centre of his body. Biggest possible target. Bang. Kick in the shoulder. Whiff of cordite. Bolt up, back, forward, down. Empty cartridge case jumps out, smoking. Down goes target. Looking rather unhappy.

The Japanese scrambled for cover on the naked hill, wriggling behind the tiniest folds in the ground, curling their legs beneath them, hunching their shoulders. But it only made the shooting of them that much easier. Stationary targets instead of mobile ones.

Now the Japanese brought up mortars. Two men came into view, struggling, their bodies angled out to take the weight of the weapon they dragged along between them.

One of the mortar-bearers fell, shot. The mortar toppled over on to his sprawled body, pulling his companion off his balance. He struggled to his feet and, perplexed, scratched his head. He looked for all the world like an Oriental Stan Laurel.

'Look at the daft sod!' Kerr yelled delightedly. 'Gormless as they come! Isn't anyone going to shoot him?' A Highlander obliged. 'That's the way to do it,' cried Kerr with a hoot of triumph.

Out of sight near the crashed Zero, a second mortar opened up. It cracked sharply; there was a puff of smoke; the bomb flew. Then: anti-climax. It didn't reach its objective. It walloped into the slope, closer to the attackers than the defenders.

The air reeked of explosive. It was a good smell, a winning smell. Men grinned in the warmth of their success and were unafraid of the bullets whirring above them like mad insects.

Kerr was everywhere. The great hulk of him would

suddenly materialize beside a nineteen-year-old rifleman. 'Be a good lad and pip that Jap down there for me, will you?' The rifleman would oblige. 'That's it! Grand, grand! The daft buggers, they don't know when they've had enough!'

The George Formby voice. Lad to lad. Professionals. Equals discussing a matter of mutual interest.

Everything was quiet on the east and west faces, according to the crackling voice on the field telephone. Cornish passed the intelligence on to Kerr who nodded, sweating and happy.

Another mortar bomb hit the slope below the road.

'They'll have to move that mortar up a bit closer,' Kerr observed, professionally interested in the enemy's problems. 'If they don't, they'll not get the range. But if they come any closer we can pick off the mortar-men before they stick their bombs down the spout.' He chuckled and breathed noisily on his glasses before polishing them with a clean white handkerchief. 'The lads are doing well, aren't they?'

'Very well,' said Cornish. 'But if you don't mind my saying so, you are taking far too many risks.'

Kerr shrugged, smiling. 'It's my job to take risks. I found out a long, long time ago that nothing gives the troops confidence like seeing their C.O. getting shot at! It's very good for morale! These lads are just beginning to feel like real soldiers. They've found out what it's like to stop running and to give the enemy a bloody nose. They're shooting well. Notice that? That's because they feel a bit of confidence in their veins. Confidence makes a man hold his rifle a bit steadier and take aim a bit more carefully.' He winked. 'If seeing me get shot at adds to that confidence, well, it's worth the risk, isn't it, when you stop to think about it.'

Worth the risk ... gamble one's life for a spot of confidence ... to enable men to hang on a little longer to a nameless hill in the jungle ... No, Cornish wanted to say, it's not worth it, not to me.

Instead he said, 'Let's hope your luck holds, sir.'

'Kind of you to say so.'

'It was partly selfish,' said Cornish. 'If you get killed, presumably I become C.O. Frankly the thought petrifies me.'

Kerr nodded, still watching the action on the slope. 'I know how you feel. I was a bit petrified myself.'

'You were?'

'Aye. Suddenly thrust into command. It came as a bloody shock, I can tell you.'

'You concealed it awfully well.'

'Well, that's the whole idea, isn't it?'

The firing eased. Again the Japanese had been stopped. The British riflemen, sweating, ragged, relaxed and savoured the sight of the enemy pulling back, in retreat, frustrated. So much for his bloody invincibility.

It was almost dark. Heavy clouds hung over the hill like an angry roof. The air seemed more liquid than gas; it stuck to you as you breathed it in; it filled you up like ginger beer.

Then the rain started. A few great drops thudded down, followed almost immediately by the deluge. The raindrops were like bullets. Nothing could keep you dry in such a downpour. It was almost solid. All you could do was huddle and hope. And listen to it exploding on your tin hat and watch it streaming off the brim. You might struggle down into your groundsheet but the rain would find its way down your neck and it would gather in pools in your lap and in your boots.

As the last light of day vanished, the rain became colder.

At first it was pleasant; beautiful, cooling fluid. But it kept on cooling. Persistently, relentlessly. Quickly your body heat plummeted. Soon you were longing for the heat of the day. You couldn't stop shivering. You rued the day you—and everyone else—had been so keen on having the regimental tailor snip off the anti-mosquito turn-ups on your shorts, to improve the way they hung. The turn-ups would have been a blessing now; but now it was too late.

It rained until midnight. Then the rain stopped. The temperature rose again.

11

During the night the Japs brought mortars close to the road. They opened fire at a few minutes past four, the first shot killing two men brewing tea.

'The trouble with mortars,' Kerr declared, 'is that you can't hear the bloody things coming, not like ordinary artillery, there's a bit of a whoosh, you know. And mortar wounds are nasty too, very nasty. Hot as hell, the shrapnel from a mortar. Bloody stuff tears a hole in a feller, then proceeds to roast him from the inside out.'

Cornish followed him into a trench. He felt the new mud squelching into his boots. He leant against the wall of the trench and it gave slightly; it was like a great slimy animal. He shivered.

I'm really not cut out for this type of work, he thought sadly. Kerr was burbling away to some wide-eyed private about Knaresborough.

'Aye, a lovely castle there. I remember walking up the hill and looking down at the river. Now, what's the name of it?'

'The Nidd, sir. The River Nidd.'

'That's it! The Nidd. A grand bridge there too. Some old fortune-teller said that when that bridge fell down, the world would come to an end.'

'Aye, it was Mother Shipton, sir.'

'Right, lad!'

Cornish folded his arms and gripped them achingly hard to stop the trembling. The rain seemed to have penetrated his body, filled his veins and soaked his bones. A near miss cracked against the slope above the trench. Sodden chunks of muck rained down on the men's helmets and shoulders.

'I thought old Mother Shipton's words had come true then,' said Kerr with a chuckle. 'Eh, Dave?'

Cornish nodded dutifully. Kerr grinned. It suddenly struck Cornish that Kerr was actually enjoying himself. It was no act, no carefully staged performance to achieve a desired effect. It was genuine. The man revelled in all this. Standing in mud like syrup. Soaked. In imminent danger of being blown to bits. He derived pleasure from it. Was it a form of masochism? Cornish blinked. It was as if he had never really seen Kerr before. In a way, he thought, he and I don't belong to quite the same species. He found himself staring at Kerr, studying the big, florid face, the busy, happy eyes. The bastard was having the time of his life.

Kerr was chatting with a corporal when the next near-miss landed. He barely paused. Cornish wondered at the man's nerves. Could he switch them off at will so that he might ignore their signals? Or did he possess no nerves? Perhaps he was unable to feel fear, just as some people are unable to feel pain.

When dawn broke, the Japanese tanks were still parked at the side of the road, snug to the non-existent kerb, as if their owners had just popped into the tobacconist's for twenty Player's. Were the Japs planning to use the tanks? Cornish remembered the Bofors anti-aircraft gun wound down to fire horizontally at oncoming Jap tanks. The shells had found their targets but they had bounced off; they had been far too light for the job. In the end the Jap tanks had simply run over the Bofors emplacement, squashing it.

Porson had been hit. He sat against a fallen tree, his hands feebly pressing on a savage stomach wound. Blood kept bubbling up around his fingers. His eyes were bright with shock. He was apologetic; he shook his head ... awfully sorry ... causing so much trouble ... letting the team down ... poor show ... He wanted to tell Kerr something else but he wasn't given the time. His eyes glazed. His lungs emptied with a spluttering and gurgling. His head sagged to one side, hair plastered in sad little curls on his forehead.

Mike Gibbs grimaced as he saw Porson. He reached out and opened the man's upper eyelid. Too late. Pupils dilated. No pulse. Man officially Deceased.

Tom Byrne came slithering over the mud, in time to say a prayer over the body.

Wearily Cornish turned away. He was sick of seeing bodies and hearing prayers about departed souls and sins being washed away. What sins, for God's sake? He watched Kerr striding along the road, his sturdy figure framed by shattered huts. The man *was* enjoying himself: you could see it in his movements, in the bounce of his feet, the swing of his arm. Having grand time. Wish you were here ...

Tom Byrne put on his ridiculous *sola topi*.

'How are you, David?'

'I'm pissed off, actually.' At once Cornish regretted the reply. It wasn't fair. Tom hadn't created this stinking mess. 'Sorry, old boy,' he said. Tom smiled. Then Cornish found himself smiling also. In that silly pith helmet and robe, Tom looked like a Victorian explorer about to take a bath.

Cornish asked Tom whether Porson was already in heaven.

'I don't know.'

'My grandfather had a picture on his upstairs landing. It was some artist's idea of heaven. A bunch of plump and rather disagreeable-looking angels strolling around on puffy white clouds playing harps. It looked bloody dull. I hope for poor old Porson's sake it's a bit more lively than that.'

'I think Porson's heaven might be precisely what Porson wants it to be.'

'He wasn't old enough to know what he wanted.'

'I doubt that age is that important, David.'

Cornish rubbed the loose flesh on either side of his brow. It seemed to ease the ache in his head. 'You really believe it, don't you?'

Tom laughed. 'Of course I do.'

'In spite of all ... *this*, you still think there's a dear, benevolent old gent beaming down on us.'

'But the point, David, is that suffering isn't a total evil. And it isn't incompatible with happiness.'

'Tell Porson's mother and father that.'

'I would if I was able. He's found peace, David.'

'He's just a chunk of smelly meat.'

'His soul is free. He is content. I know it. I've seen it again and again. When a man is dying he finds peace. Just before the end he seems to see what is around the next corner and suddenly he doesn't resent being taken. In fact, he's happy....'

'Hey!'

'Here they come!'

Voices shrill with disbelief. Harsh with dismay. Men scrambled to their feet, working the bolts of their rifles. With a smile and a tiny bow of farewell, Tom Byrne tipped his pith helmet and wished Cornish a very good day.

The Japs swarmed up the hill as the mortar bombs still fell. In the fresh loveliness of the dawn hour they blew bugles and whistles and shouted to one another and pushed on toward the British positions. And fell. And died. They had guts; you could hate them but you had to admire them. Endless clips of rounds disappeared into piping-hot magazines. Arms, leaden with fatigue, levelled and fired and reloaded and fired the venerable Lee Enfields.

It was like a film seen over and over again. The same men seemed to be coming into view, the same officers waving swords and exhorting their poor devils of men to God only knows what new effort. The same men toppled and fell and bled and beat the ground with angry fists; the same bodies slithered and rolled down the pitiless slope.

The assault went on. Doggedly the Japanese infantry plodded into hails of lead. Had they been attacking on level ground there seems little doubt that they would have swarmed over the British positions in short order. But it was hard enough to stand upright on the slippery incline, let alone charge. Try as they might the Japanese could maintain no impetus in their attacks.

But the men who died provided cover for those who survived. As the attacks faltered, the infantry went to earth behind comrades' bodies and established a line of sorts only a few score yards from the British. But it was a broken, unprofessional line. The Japanese soon abandoned it and returned to the valley.

The Tommies snatched sleep whenever they could. They simply closed their eyes, some with their fingers still on the trigger, and were transported to unlikely places where there were women whose soft arms were clean and fresh.

Cornish slept for two hours. He hadn't consciously closed his eyes but he awoke to find that he had been half leaning, half lying against the lashed tree-trunks. His revolver had fallen from his hands and lay on the scarred wood before him.

I suppose I could be shot at dawn for sleeping on duty, he thought. He was brightly awake now; he felt as if he had slept the clock round. Nerves a-pound, heart a-thump.

The sky was clear now, the sun bright and hot.

On the slope a wounded man sobbed in a hopeless way.

Cornish sat up. It occurred to him that he was leading

a thoroughly unhealthy life, in turn roasted and frozen, soaked and steamed. And getting insufficient sleep.

Two of Mike Gibbs' orderlies were removing the body of a rifleman, a slim fellow with very fair hair. He had been shot in the head. The poor chap must have died without anyone noticing, Cornish thought. It seemed a particularly sad way to go.

'Fisher, sir,' said one of the orderlies.

'Oh yes, Fisher.'

On the slope, like slugs, lay the Japanese dead. In the jungle, a vile-voiced creature screeched.

There was the sound of a motor being started. Cornish looked quickly into the valley. Yes, a puff of exhaust smoke from the leading tank:

Christ, thought Cornish, his guts twisting within him. He beckoned to a corporal.

'My compliments to Major Kerr,' he said, 'and would you ask him if he would kindly join me here.'

Some daft sod fired a shot.

Kerr scowled. 'Tell that man not to waste his ammo!'

Behind him someone repeated the order.

Cornish was breathing heavily. Kerr glanced at him. He looked a bit grey, did Mr Cornish. The younger man's eyes were on the two tanks that came waddling up the hill.

'They're Ninety-Fives, all right,' said Kerr, but Cornish only nodded. He didn't seem to be in the most conversational of moods.

The tanks were labouring on the incline. Their caterpillar tracks kept slithering on the loose stones. They made progress, nevertheless; they came nearer.

Formidable looking monsters. Kerr sniffed. You had to keep reminding yourself they had men in them.

'Everyone know what to do? Any last-minute questions?'

The men nodded and shook their heads. And set their shoulders. Kerr turned to them, grinned. 'All right, let's be about it then!'

Hurriedly, the party made for the sharp bend in the road where it turned from the hill to enter the *kampong*. There they took up their individual positions.

The first tank stopped. The barrel of its gun swept from left to right and back again like an evil wand. The barrel was depressed to compensate for the incline but the angle was still wrong. The tank would have to come nearer.

Kerr beckoned to it, luring it on. He could feel his heart thumping against his ribs. He was grinning fiercely but he wasn't aware of it.

The leading tank began to move again, groaning at the effort, a lazy crustacean prodded into motion.

'Bit farther, come on, come on!'

'I don't think he can see it,' said Cornish, his eyes riveted on the tank, 'not from that angle.' His hands were clasping air.

'Christ, he's stopped again!'

The bastard. There he was, just a yard away from where he was supposed to be.

Again the turret traversed and the great barrel swept the scene before it.

Kerr wondered what the Jap gunner could see from that angle. A bit of the village, probably, but not the trenches.

Cornish said, 'Do you think we should have a go now, sir?'

'No. Wait.'

There was a machine-gun beneath the cannon; its barrel looked slight and insignificant. But it wasn't hard to imagine what it could do to the party if they attempted to run now.

Suddenly the cannon barrel recoiled. A crack. The tank

rocked. Two hundred yards down the road, a hut was transformed into flying fragments.

'Daft bugger. What's the good of that?'

'I really don't know,' said Cornish.

Kerr smiled to himself; he hadn't expected an answer. Another shot. A tree collapsed.

Silence.

Kerr said to the tank: 'You daft bugger. You've got to get nearer if you're going to do any good at all.'

And, with a screech and a roar, the tank jolted into motion.

And tumbled head first twenty feet through the false surface of stones on branches, into the pit. It stuck there, its engine screaming, its tracks whirring in impotent fury.

Cornish glanced quickly back. Dead white beneath his tan. Mouth a little straight line.

Kerr nodded. 'Yes, go on—now!'

The squad dashed forward, clutching grenades and rifles and steel bars removed from the Bedfords. They knew what to do for they had rehearsed. Their boots slithered excitedly on the loose stones. One man slipped; he dropped a couple of grenades which bounced on the springy grass. A comrade grabbed the man by the shoulder before he fell. The men hurled themselves on the tank as if bent on consuming it. They jammed grenades under the hatch locks, pulled the pins, ducked away. The detonations boomed against the tank's steel hull.

Suddenly, Kerr remembered the second tank. It took a moment to find it. He laughed. It was heading away down the hill at full tilt.

Sergeant Firmin lobbed a grenade through the now-open hatch on top of the turret. A second man quickly slammed the lid shut and leant his weight on it. Kerr beamed. Grand, teamwork; you couldn't beat it. . . .

The 7.7 mm machine-gun had been blazing away at the bottom of the pit, the rounds thudding uselessly into the soft mud. Probably the poor devil of a gunner couldn't see anything else to shoot at because of the tank's attitude. When Firmin's grenade exploded with a pleasantly hollow-sounding bang, the shooting stopped.

'That's got the bastards,' said someone.

Kerr clambered on to the tank's body. Firmin threw open the hatch-lid. Inside, the three-man crew lay torn and crushed. The air was foul with explosive and gases from torn bodies. It looked like the pillbox at Thiepval Wood, the trench at Lens, the O.P. at Vimy. Sometimes our lot, sometimes theirs. Comrade or enemy, Oriental or Occidental, the same grotesque attitudes, squashed faces, mouths agape with screams never uttered, eyes grey with death.

The steel of the tank's hull was warm beneath his hands. The men grinned as they looked up at him. Triumphal grins. Grins full of pride. Grins of men who had stopped retreating.

The second tank was at the bottom of the hill. It turned as if to say farewell to its companion.

Odd lot, the Japs, Kerr thought, they throw away men's lives but they're bloody misers with their tanks.

Riches beyond one's wildest dreams.

More than a hundred rounds of ammunition for the cannon—which was in excellent working order—and well over 2,000 rounds for the two machine-guns, one of which still worked.

The tank itself could not be started. The grenades had crippled its 110-horsepower diesel beyond repair. It was possible, however, to dig another trench behind the tank and lever it with tree-trunks held by sweating, straining men. Agonizingly, they kept nudging its ten leaden tons until

97

it had turned round and faced the Japanese.

Milne, in deference to his artillery associations, was given the task of sorting out how to operate the cannon.

Five minutes later the first shot was fired. It burst in the jungle with a thoroughly satisfying bang, an eruption of smoke and a tumbling of a tree or two. The troops cheered.

Milne gave two men a brief course in the firing of the cannon. The team fired a couple of dozen shots at the enemy before breaking for tea.

But the Japanese fired back. They had the tank in view and they were clearly anxious to knock it out. Before Milne and his two assistants had finished their tea, they succeeded.

The wreckage of the tank burned into the night, the machine-gun ammunition exploding with vicious little cracks, the cannon shells going off with sharper, louder cracks.

If you really wanted to cheese yourself off you could count the rounds as they burst.

At dawn, the artillery opened up again. The shells cracked into the hill in angry procession. The noise was appalling. You gasped for breath because it seemed to swallow the air. You clenched your teeth because you thought the din would tear your jaws apart. You buried your face in the dirt, reacting like any sensible creature; you tried to wriggle your way back into the womb of the earth.

Dust to flaming dust.

When the artillery ceased, the Japanese infantry again carried their rifles and their swords up the hill. Once more they chose the direct route. Once more they staggered under a curtain of bullets. Once more they fell and bled and died. Sheer courage wasn't enough. One man, a corporal, actually reached the British positions. He had three bullets in him but he managed to pull himself over the lip of a trench.

A rifleman named Anderson watched him for two or three seconds. He felt almost sorry for the poor sod, he looked so done in. Then he shot him and his head snapped back, suddenly bubbling red. The Jap corporal's body slumped loosely on the slope like a sack of potatoes.

The corporal's death was like a signal. The attack faltered. Here and there a valiant man tried to keep it going, but the spirit was gone. Once more the Japanese fell back. A heavy silence descended. Soon the sky darkened and a brief but ferocious rain squall drenched the slope, washing away some of the blood.

Exhausted, the British troops laid down their rifles and wrapped themselves in rotting groundsheets still wet from the last rain. The men's feet were under water—so bloody what? Their heads rested on mud—to hell with the mud. The bloke next-but-one got his lot—tough titty. Utter fatigue brought the realization that the ammo was being used up at a fearful rate—and so were the troops ... and if they were going to get help through, they'd better get a bloody move on because if they left it too long, they'd be too late. As usual.

Then Kerr would appear. With reassurances galore.

12

Life began to assume a lunatic sort of order. A brew-up, for example, could be expected every few hours provided the Japs weren't actually assaulting the hill. One man would put a few pints of petrol in a biscuit tin, a second would fill the brewing-can (another biscuit tin) with water. A match dropped into the petrol tin produced a fierce blaze; on went the brewing-tin; soon the water was boiling. In went a packet of tea followed by the contents of a tin of evaporated milk and a couple of handfuls of sugar. The result was hot and sickly and totally wrong for this climate and this place —but absolutely right for these men. Brew-ups continued even when the supplies of evaporated milk and sugar ran out. Tea was tea, even when black and bitter.

In lulls, the Japanese fired one mortar every four minutes. Precisely four minutes. Someone dubbed it the Four-Minute Egg. It was exhausting and infuriating, having to prepare oneself for the arrival of the beastly thing.

One of the mortar bombs failed to explode on impact. It landed in a trench, missing the left shoulder of Private Harding, W.F., by no more than half a dozen inches. It stuck in the trench wall behind him, its tail protruding. Harding reached out and touched the bomb. It exploded, killing him and badly injuring seven other men.

There was no toothpaste on the hill. Not much soap. Little bread. No butter. There were, however, adequate stocks of bully beef, tinned fruit and, for some reason, HP sauce. A case of Brasso still sat in the back of a lorry. Beside it were twelve gross of bootlaces.

Water was plentiful, obtainable from a spring on the west face, although its quality was questioned by some men with heaving bowels.

There were twelve dozen pairs of puttees, neatly bundled and tied with string, six packets of forms on which M.T. officers could detail the precise petrol consumption of H.M. vehicles, twelve dozen electric light bulbs (four dozen 25-watt and the balance 60-watt), fifty small cartons each containing 1,000 staples and a cardboard box packed with twelve dozen bottles of blue-black ink.

No one knew why these items had been loaded on the lorries, or who had loaded them.

Kerr established himself in what he called his cave. Actually it was little more than an angular indentation in the slope immediately above the road a hundred yards from the *kampong*, or what was left of the *kampong*.

McGregor had industriously shored the cave with planks torn from native huts; he had made a floor of bits of *atap*. There was room for a battered Malayan bamboo chair rescued from a burning hut. A couple of ammunition boxes created a table of sorts—which, McGregor explained, could also serve as a foot-rest. A solitary candle provided illumination. Outside, half buried, a blackened and ugly section of the Japanese tank's hull protected the entrance of the cave from blast.

From his bamboo chair, Kerr could see many of his men. They were a bedraggled, grubby-looking lot; but there was an air about them, a stubborn air. The longer they held the hill the more determined they became to continue holding it. The hill was theirs and, much as they might hate the sight of it, they weren't planning to let the Japs have it. Soldiers have a way of becoming possessive about the positions they hold, Kerr thought, which is just as bloody well for their officers.

The few bits of tobacco left in his pouch were dry. Gathered and packed they constituted only half a fill. And rather a hot and bitter fill at that. No matter, it was a delectable smoke because it was the last smoke.

No more tobacco. Or brandy.

What was left was hardly a tot. A mouthful, to be gently shifted around with the tongue, to lap over every tooth and into every corner: a farewell tour of the place.

Louise liked brandy. Liked? *Adored* was nearer the mark. She had a passionate love affair with the stuff. Of course, it was the boy's death that did it. Kerr frowned, remembering. Poor little bastard was run over by a bus. His pram ran away; brakes didn't hold properly or hadn't been put on properly; it was never determined. It was all over in a few seconds. Bonny little chap, he was. He would have been over twenty now. He might even have been here, on this hill, helping his old dad fight the Japs. Brian, a man, a soldier, a subaltern perhaps, probably with an Oxford accent like Cornish, a damn sight more of a gentleman than his dad, handsome, a wicked one with the girls....

Oh hell, there was nothing to be gained by thinking of what might have been. What did happen was that his wife became a professional drinker. The bitch, she hardly drew a sober breath from the day Brian died to the day she was good enough to do the same. It took her eighteen years. She worked hard at it, he had to hand her that much. In the end she weighed not much more than five stone. An evil-tongued, evil-smelling husk of a woman. She blamed him, somehow or other, for what happened; yet he was in Catterick at the time, on a training course. But it was no use trying to tell her that; it was never any use trying to tell her anything.

In spite of all that, if it hadn't been for Louise, his army career would undoubtedly have been a short one. He would have become a commercial traveller or a bank clerk or something equally horrible.

He met Louise Hatton on a train which had just passed Stoke-on-Trent. It was a Monday evening in January 1918. He was journeying home on leave, freshly endowed with King George V's commission as a second-lieutenant in the Armed Forces Of The Empire. His uniform was splendidly new, his Sam Browne stiff and glittering. He had seven days' leave, after which he had to return to France. It seemed highly likely that he would be dead by the end of February, according to the experts' statistics on the life expectancy of subalterns on the Western Front. Subalterns died in their dozens because they were the leaders of every futile, ill-planned assault that the Staff ordered. They stood on the sandbags in full view of the enemy machine-gunners and waved their revolvers and blew their whistles and led their platoons across the foulness of No-Man's land. Their tunics, their collars and ties, their natty breeches: all were symbols of rank which made them prime targets for the well-practised German gunners. Thus subalterns were in short supply. Qualifications were lowered drastically; by late 1917, even men with council-school educations might be considered if they displayed qualities of leadership and weren't *too* gross of manner and speech.

Kerr hadn't hesitated when the opportunity of a commission came his way. He was conscious, but only in an abstract way, of his chances of survival as an officer. Somehow it was hard to think much beyond being kitted out and having sergeants saluting and being seen in Rochdale, Albert Kerr's boy. A lad simply couldn't turn down such an opportunity, even if it did seem quite likely to kill him.

Seven days. Not a moment to waste. The girl in the blue dress had boarded at the last station and had sat beside him in the only vacant seat. A thoroughly gradely bit of crackling. Lady-like but with a sexy mouth. Blue eyes set very wide apart. A lovely straight nose. Far, far beyond the aspirations of a common *non*-com, of course.

Right. No time to dilly. Or dally. He smiled to himself. First, feign yawn. Second, close novel. Third, pretend to doze. A minute later the book slid sideways from his lap. Instantly awake, he apologized profusely. Had the book bruised her? Books could be right sharp, couldn't they? Especially the edges.

She smiled at him. Her gaze was steady, however. She wasn't fooled for a moment, she seemed to say, but she was willing to exchange a few words with the young officer because he was moderately handsome and possessed of a certain charm. What, she wanted to know, was the name of the book that had almost caused her grievous bodily harm?

'*Of Human Bondage*,' he told her. 'A feller called Somerset Maugham wrote it.'

'I know,' she said. 'I understand it's rather daring.'

'Aye, it is that. Quite daring.' He paused only a moment. 'Where are you getting off? If you don't mind my asking.'

'Manchester,' she said. 'My aunt is meeting me.'

He glanced at her hands—exquisitely tiny but sheathed in black kid. 'You're not married or anything are you?'

She frowned; her eyes lost their warmth. 'You don't waste time, lieutenant—or rather, *second*-lieutenant.'

The train began to slow.

Kerr cleared his throat. 'I'm going to Rochdale,' he announced, grimly aware of the interest of the flannel-faced old

cow in the seat opposite. 'It's not that far from Manchester.'
'Really.' Christ, now she was turning coolish, right coolish. Not encouraging.
'Only half an hour by tram.' Damn! 'Less by taxi.'
'I see.'

Hell, the train had almost reached London Road Station. And she was turning to ice! Had she suddenly made up her mind that he was nothing but a common ranker disguised as a gentleman? Had he ruined everything by mentioning a *tram*? Or was Rochdale the problem? Was Rochdale one of those *ghastly* places the other officer cadets had sometimes mentioned?

The other passengers were already on their feet, lurching as they heaved cases from the overhead racks.

Kerr thought rapidly. Advance at the double, lad, he told himself; there's no other way. 'As Rochdale is so close to Manchester,' he said, 'it'll be that much easier for me to nip over and see you.'

'And why,' she enquired, clearly enjoying his discomfiture, 'would you want to "nip" over and see me?'

He looked boldly into those calm blue eyes. 'You know bloody well why,' he said distinctly. Around him, above him, heads turned, shocked. He ignored them. He was busy watching her as she bit gently into her smiling lower lip. The train halted with a gasp and a squeal. A strand of hair strayed across her forehead in a quite erotic way. 'Thirty Marina Avenue,' she said. 'Wednesday. Say seven.'

It was a tumultuous leave, a topsy-turvy leave. His world came to pieces which promptly re-assembled themselves in a new and utterly wonderful order. Never before had he encountered anyone remotely like Louise Hatton. She was beautiful, intelligent, splendidly unafraid of pinch-lipped conventions; she wanted to know all the dirty stories from the Front; she could match every one with one of her own.

Her father, it transpired, was a colonel of cavalry who had been waiting since August 1914 for the order to lead his dragoons in glorious charge. Louise lived with her mother in Bishop's Stortford. She admitted that she was 'sort of semi-engaged' to an R.F.C. pilot—and no longer a virgin. It had happened, she explained with disarming candour, during the airman's last leave, in July. Seven times—actually eight, if what might be termed a misfire was included. An ulcer of jealousy erupted inside Kerr. But it wasn't long before he had forgiven her; it wasn't her fault; it was that swinish aviator; they were all the same.

The widowed aunt went one afternoon to do her bit rolling bandages at the military hospital.

'You will be a darling and take it out in time, won't you?'

And later:

'I say, Ernest, you really do that awfully well.'

'Thank you.'

'You must have had lots of practice.'

'Only eight times, including what might be termed a misfire,' he said mockingly.

She laughed. 'Run your fingers very lightly up there and over there and around here.'

'I love your body, every last square inch of it. It's perfect.'

'So are you. You're beautiful. And so is he, except that he looks so small and shrivelled.'

'He's resting between rounds.'

'I don't like him to rest.'

'He has to. You're wonderfully hairy, for a girl.'

'That doesn't sound very nice.'

'It is. You have it all in one spot. It's grand.'

'"Grand". What an adorable term!'

'You have miraculous breasts. I particularly like the way your nipples are almost flat at the tips. That's a sure sign.'

'Of what?'

'I can't tell you. I'm an officer and a gentleman.'
'I think he's showing signs of life again.'
'No wonder, you doing that.'
'Ernest.'
'Yes, love.'
'Do remember to take him out in time, won't you?'

In the summer, while the Second Battle of the Marne raged, Kerr and Louise Hatton were married, despite energetic opposition from her people. Surely she could see that, admirable chap though he was, he was, well, rather 'unsuitable' ... background distinctly 'unimpressive' ... really no education worth talking about ... no family and, God knows, no prospects. (Meanwhile the R.F.C. pilot had ceased to be a problem, having collided with a DFW biplane over Amiens.) Kerr's relatives were, in their own way, as dismayed as Colonel and Mrs Hatton. Louise, they declared, was a lovely lass ... but not 'our sort' ... and o'erstepping one's class always brought grief in the end because no matter what, class always 'told'.

Nevertheless, the marriage of Lieutenant E. G. Kerr and Miss Louise Enid Hatton did take place. And four months and twelve days later, the war ended. In spite of the experts and the Germans, Kerr had survived it. It was a fact to be considered and wondered about again and again. It took some sinking in. All of a sudden he had a future to think about.

13

Yet another attack. Bullets sped and found homes in flesh and bone or flew wide to tumble among the leaves and vines of the jungle, to be stared at inquisitively by animals, to be sniffed, to be left to corrode, to return to the elements from which they were made.

Men wondered numbly at how emotionless they had become about killing. Almost without thought, they jammed clips of cartridges into the magazines of their rifles and thrust home the bolts and slung the stocks into their shoulders and levelled off fore and aft sights. And fired. The death of men was a kind of mass-production business. The enemy were targets; for as long as it seemed possible to remember, they had been trying to scale the hill; for as long as it seemed possible to remember, the defenders had been shooting them down.

Half the defenders' ammunition had been expended.

There was some fresh fruit, coconuts and a few bananas. Some of the soldiers boiled the cabbage-like leaves they found growing behind the *kampong*. The result had a dull taste but it seemed harmless. Sweet potatoes were tasty; it was essential to boil them, however, if a particularly painful stomach-ache was to be avoided. A private named Philips discovered that the large Malayan snails made a passable snack. He cracked the shells, cut away the intestines and boiled the muscular 'foot'. For some time only the most adventurous gourmets would dare consume the things; then the word got around that in spite of their unwholesome appearance, the snails were quite palatable; they tasted rather like unsalty shell fish and were a welcome change from bully beef. From then on, it was a major accomplishment to find a snail on the hill.

On the south slope, orderlies built crude shelters of *atap* to shield the wounded from the sun and rain. Mike Gibbs, the M.O., worked hard, but patients died needlessly because of the shortage of almost every form of medical supply. And Gibbs slept after eighteen or twenty hours' work while men whimpered and groaned in pain. He said he had to sleep. If he didn't, he would become ill and unable to do anything for anyone. Since he was the only doctor, he said, it was his duty to keep himself in running order.

Through it all, Kerr seemed utterly contemptuous of the Japanese and their firepower. He was the sinew of the unit's morale; without him the enemy would have been twice as numerous and determined. There was universal agreement that there had never been anyone quite so daft—and yet so grand. There was little doubt that at some point in the very near future he was going to get his lot; but secretly every man liked to think Ernie Kerr inviolable.

The aircraft came from the east, sleek twin-engined jobs. They sped over the jungle in two flights of three.

The word flashed: Blenheims! Ours! Here at last were the supplies and reinforcements...!

But hope died as the aircraft broke formation and circled the hill. Great red discs adorned their mottled bodies and wings.

Japs. Mitsubishis, someone said. They turned in the sun, examining their targets from all angles before attacking.

The raspy sound of the Japanese engines dinned in every ear. The faces of the aircrews could be glimpsed through shimmering windows as the aircraft sped by.

'Look out!'

'Duck!'

The first bombs wobbled into space. For a moment or two their fall was positively leisurely; they seemed to glide, their bodies parallel to the path of the bomber. Only when they had fallen some distance did they assume a more meaningful angle, noses slanting down, tails jogged by the streaming air. Just before they landed, they were in a vertical position.

Cornish watched the bombs smack into the hill, becoming fountains of spraying dirt and smoke. He grimaced at the sight of two men spinning like insects flicked from a bare arm. One man had lost a leg; his path through the air seemed awkward and ill-balanced. The other man turned steadily as he rose and fell; he bounced grotesquely as he hit the ground. A bomb landed in the centre of the *kampong*; another exploded in a packed trench.

Cornish lay hugging the earth as the hot air tore over him. His fingers thrust themselves into the mud as if each was seeking protection independently.

He cursed the Japanese bombers. Swines, bastards... His vocabulary was pitifully inadequate.

The world buckled and shivered. Somewhere a man screamed—or was it a creature from the jungle? The air was sour with the stink of explosives. Now the rattle of machine-guns mingled with the roar of the bombers' engines. The pilots were permitting their gunners to demonstrate their marksmanship on the decadent English targets. Round and round the mulberry bush... rat-a-tatter-tatter. Even their damned machine-guns sounded Oriental. Cornish winced as a bomber swept over him, tiny lights flickering at machine-gun muzzles. Bullets thudded into wood, into earth, into flesh. A bomb fell on the road. It made a sharper, angrier bang than those that fell on the soft earth. An arm, still bearing the armband with corporal's chevrons, spun through the air and came to rest entangled in the branches of a tree.

'Use the Brens!' Cornish ordered. 'Hurry!'

A bomber dinned overhead, not more than fifty feet up. It had a white band around the fuselage near the tail and a red arrow-like device painted on the fin; oil-stains smeared the underside of the wings behind the engines.

Cornish levelled his revolver and fired, once, twice.

'Hard luck, sir,' said Corporal Hall. He sounded like a man at a fairground rifle-range. Have another go, do, guv'nor; next time you'll win the big prize....

'So they've had to bring their bloody air force to help them out!'

It was Kerr, squinting disdainfully at the bombers, his arms folded, his legs astride. Totally unafraid.

Suddenly there was a bomber swooping down at him, guns flashing.

'Look out! Behind you!'

'What?'

It sounded ridiculous, warning a man about a twin-engined bomber as one might warn him about an errant bicycle in a playground. And it might as well have been left unsaid, because Kerr took no notice. He only turned to talk to the men in the trench. Above, bullets sizzled through leaves and struck branches. The din was appalling as the bomber hurtled overhead. A man's face could be seen in one of the machine's windows. He was a gunner and he looked directly at Kerr and cursed himself for having missed him.

Kerr glanced back at him.

'Noisy bastard.'

A man laughed nervously. Good old Ernie.

Kerr said, 'Reminds me of a mother-in-law I once had.' He sniffed comically. The George Formby voice once more: all pals together: all sharing the same minor irritation: all putting the best face on it until the minor irritation goes away.

Then someone said, 'Ah...!' as if personally feeling the impact of the bullet. Cornish turned in time to see a man sprawling full length on the road. He had been carrying ammo to the Brens when he had been hit; cartridges were bouncing on the road like ping-pong balls.

'It's Sims,' said someone.

'Here, hold this, lad.' Kerr thrust his swagger-stick into a private's hand. He was out of the trench in a moment, hurrying across to Sims. Simultaneously another Japanese bomber came roaring over the crest of the hill. Anger and fear struck at Cornish's heart as he pulled himself up the muddy, slimy wall of the trench. Greater stupidity hath no man than he give up his life for another...

Bullets whacked into the road only inches from his clutching fingers. Spat... spat... spat. He felt the shocked air recoiling from the bullets. He let go. And slumped awkwardly back into the trench.

'You hit, sir?' Firmin. Anxious, stupid face.

'No... nearly, though... bloody nearly.'

He got to his feet, his head reeling with the din and the fright of it all. What about Kerr? Christ, he must have been hit. Head up; have a look. It required a distinct order to himself to make himself stand up and look. Then, frightened, he ducked again. No, thank God, it was only a bird, poor bloody thing, flying an erratic, panicky flight across the hill.

Kerr returned, half dragging, half carrying Sims.

'Poor lad, he's badly hurt, I'm afraid.'

Hands took Sims's limp body.

'It's all right, sir, we got 'im.'
'Are you sure?'
'Yes sir, come on down, sir, gimme your 'and.'
Kerr smiled at Cornish. 'All right, Dave?'
'Me? Yes, of course, sir.'
'Poor feller got one in the belly.'
Awkwardly, Cornish said the rescue was a good show.
Kerr shrugged and took his swagger-stick from the private who had been holding it.
Awe shone in the man's eyes. He fumbled in his pockets and found a cigarette and offered it to Kerr. 'Will you take it, sir? I'd like you to ... really I would.'
'That's very kind, lad. Very kind indeed, but I wouldn't dream of taking your smoke....'
'I think they're going,' barked Sergeant Firmin.
Heads turned skywards as the Mitsubishis swept down over their comrades in the jungle at the foot of the hill, their great metal wings swaying in haughty farewell.
The sounds of their engines were still reverberating as the Japanese troops attacked again.
Weary, past anger, beyond disbelief, the British turned to the slope. Couldn't the Nips give it a bloody rest? Didn't they know when enough was ruddy well enough?
But already shots were spitting over the trenches and officers and N.C.O.s were exhorting their men to look lively and not bugger about as if this was a sodding Sunday afternoon picnic because it bloody well wasn't. Stop huddling. Get organized.
Half dazed by the intensity of the Japanese air attack, the British riflemen reacted instinctively, automatically, their hands grasping for their rifles and for clips of ammunition; they took their places at the trench walls and squinted with red-rimmed eyes for a glimpse of the targets.
Lance-Corporal Alan Layton simply stared when Corporal

Hall asked him why he wasn't firing. He stared but he didn't seem to see. His eyes didn't focus on anything or anyone; his mouth was slightly open; the tip of his tongue kept running along his lower teeth. Hall grabbed his shoulder. 'C'mon, mate,' he hissed. It didn't do for any N.C.O. not to answer the call. Bad example for the troops. He told Layton to smarten up and get to it. But Lance-Corporal Layton's head just wobbled in a silly, half-witted way.

'I'm going home,' he mumbled. 'I'm not staying here; I'm going home.'

He wriggled free of Hall's grasp. Head still shaking, he pulled himself up and out of the trench. He slithered on the muddy surface, half fell, then began to pull himself to his feet again. Simultaneously four Japanese bullets hit him, two in the chest, one in the throat and one in the left arm.

'Here ... what?'

Surprised, hurt, Lance-Corporal Layton tumbled backwards and lay still, the blood pumping from his throat until there was no more to pump.

The battle was fierce, the enemy determined.

Kerr was everywhere.

'Do you think it's time to let the Bren-gunners have a go?' He stroked his chin as if he had all the time in the world to ponder the question.

Cornish said, yes, yes, anything that was available should be fired ... and fired ... and fired.

Kerr winked reassuringly as he nodded. Everything's under control, he seemed to say. Nowt to worry about. A grin.

Oh Christ, thought Cornish, as he plodded after Kerr, I think he must be off his rocker. A mortar bomb landed fifty yards away. He ducked, slipping and sprawling on the mud.

'All right, Dave, are you?'

Kerr stood upright. Unharmed. Cornish wondered why, until he saw that the blast had been deflected by the remains of a hut. Why the hell was Kerr always so bloody infuriatingly lucky? Angry at himself and at Kerr's luck, he pulled himself to his feet. He swore vilely, after which he felt a little better.

Kerr spent a few minutes with the Bren-gunners. He helped to pass out the 36-round magazines of ammunition —'Short bursts, if you don't mind, lads. Make every round count.' It amused him to carry half a dozen grenades which he would toss to his men like cricket balls. 'Here, lad, see if you can lob this into those Japs down there. See the ones I mean? Aye, that's it, the three of them. Are you a good shot? Let's see, shall we? Five pounds if you can hit him in the balls with it!'

All good sport. Cornish wanted to tell Kerr to treat the grenades with more respect. They were frightfully dangerous things. He kept seeing diagrams, cut-away drawings from manuals and text to be learnt by heart: 'Remove the safety pin so that only your grip prevents the movement of the striker lever. When the grenade is thrown, the striker lever is released, permitting movement of the striker spring. This permits the striker-head to hit the cartridge-cap setting the fuse in motion. The fuse burns from four to five seconds after which the explosive, a mixture of gelignite and cyclonite, is detonated and the outer casing, a ferrous casting, breaks into some eighty pieces. The grenade is an effective anti-personnel weapon....'

The Japanese rallied again and again, clambering to their feet and pressing on, meeting the British fire, absorbing it, taking their losses, falling like awkward little dolls that rolled and tumbled down the slope.

* * *

Time passed in a jerky, uneven way. There were moments to pause and realize that one was as hungry as hell; moments to wonder on the fact that somehow the hill was still in British hands and somehow one was still in one piece, bodily, if not mentally; moments to look about one and see if Arthur and Bill and Mike were still around; moments to recall an odd place where a missed bus was a major disaster, where people slept in between clean sheets on soft mattresses, where meals were on tables and didn't consist of bully beef and weeds, where a fellow wouldn't hear a shot fired from one year's end to the next. But then time would vanish in great chunks, three and four hours at once: hundreds of minutes lost in the hypnosis of battle. Fingers that once wrapped bacon and punched tram tickets now handled rifles with deadly skill; men who vomited at the sight of blood now killed mechanically, callously.

Despite their losses, the Japanese kept increasing their pressure on the British. Each assault brought them a few yards nearer. Sharp-eyed riflemen could have made reasonably accurate guesses as to the ages of the Japs they shot; some saw the scars on the Japs' foreheads where N.C.O.s had beaten them for misdemeanours, the sweat darkening tunics in great patches, the determination or the terror or the hate in their eyes. Sometimes their voices could be heard: shrill, urgent; sometimes they cried when the bullets hit home; sometimes they fell without a sound.

Sergeant Firmin severed the ropes with a Malayan *parang*. But the tree-trunk didn't move; it had settled itself comfortably in the soft earth. The men who had laboriously dragged it up the slope now sweated to send it down again.

'Get your feet against it!' Sergeant Firmin's voice was harsh with urgency. 'Give it a real shove, for Christ's sake!'

'Ah, it's moving,' said Cornish—and at once cursed it

for a stupidly obvious remark. The trunk was indeed moving and everyone could see that it was. With a creaking like a sailing-ship in a gale it began to roll. Ponderously at first, then alive with its own momentum, it headed down the slope. Every foot increased its speed. By the time it reached the first Jap it was fairly bounding. It jumped right over one man. Then it caught a group immediately behind him, swiping them, scattering them as if they were lead soldiers cleared from a table by an ill-tempered child.

The British riflemen thought it was the funniest sight they had seen since the night the ENSA soprano's left tit fell out on high D.

Good old Ernie. Trust him. The men automatically assumed that it was Kerr who had thought of using tree-trunks to fight Japs.

Corporal Hall said, 'Excuse me, sir. Broadbent's had it.'

'What?' Cornish looked up from the Personnel and Supply statement he was attempting to prepare.

'Broadbent, the signals bod, sir...'

'He's dead, you say?'

'Yes, sir. Blown to bits. His wireless too. Bloody shell must have landed right on him. There's just a bloody great hole, sir, where he was.'

'Then how do you know...?'

'We found a finger, sir.'

'I see. But how do you know it belongs, er, belonged to Corporal Broadbent?'

'I recognize it, sir.'

'You do?'

'Yes sir. Split nail, sir. He did it last week. He showed it to me at the time. It's his finger all right, sir.'

'Very well. I'll take your word for it.'

'Yes sir,' said Corporal Hall.

Twenty-three minutes later he was decapitated by a Four-Minute Egg.

He had written the figures with an indelible pencil on an envelope which he had received in November. You could still read the London W.1 imprint on the stamp. 'We have lost 163 men killed and 194 men wounded, not counting those with minor wounds who are staying at their posts.'

'Good lads,' said Kerr, peering out over the jungle. Dark clouds hung low, a gloomy ceiling threatening more rain. The firing was spasmodic now: a token shot every minute or so to supplement the mortars.

Cornish said, 'And slightly more than half the ammunition has been used up.'

Kerr turned, frowning. 'More than half, eh? I'm not surprised. I was wondering how it was lasting.'

'We could use what's left in two days.'

'I realize that,' said Kerr flatly. He took a deep breath of the humid air. 'So they'd better send us some more, hadn't they?'

'But we don't know whether they will. Perhaps they don't know we're here.'

'They know,' Kerr said. 'The wireless or the runners; the news must have got through somehow.'

'I wish I shared your confidence, sir.'

Kerr smiled. 'Aye, so do I.'

They walked along the path that led to the hill's southern face. No bodies, foul and bloated, on these slopes; just the ramshackle dressing station with its crazy bits of bamboo and wood.

The jungle extended all the way to Singapore. *They* were there; *they* had ammo and food and medical supplies—and planes to transport them. Were Soper and Latimer panting out the news to incredulous generals at that very moment?

Was it just a matter of hours until the sky trembled with the sound of R.A.F. planes bulging with supplies?

'But don't you think we should be prepared for the worst, just in case?'

'No,' said Kerr.

'But, sir—'

Kerr smiled. 'It's a bad habit to get into, preparing for the worst.'

'But the Japs might overrun us. It's a possibility. Surely we should have a plan to put into effect if it happens.'

Still smiling, Kerr shook his head. 'It won't happen, Dave. They won't overrun us.'

Cornish watched a large black bird turning in the sky. He envied the bird its freedom. He could think of nothing more to say to Kerr. So, he told himself, say nothing. Would it be possible to slip down the west face and escape through the jungle? How far might he get? The thought of being alone in the jungle was frightening.

So was the thought of staying on the hill.

'We're not going to think of defeat, Dave,' said Kerr. 'It's not going to cross our minds.'

Did Kerr hope the words might be remembered for the history books?

The Japanese had brought up more artillery. Heavy pieces. The hill shuddered under impact after impact. At times it seemed to vanish under a fog of dust and dirt and smoke, but it kept reappearing like a boxer who has long since lost the ability of knowing when he has absorbed enough punishment.

The British troops clung to the floors of their trenches. Some were buried alive. Others, incredibly, survived explosions within a few feet of them. Many a man cried with the strain; some defecated involuntarily. For one man, a private named Baldwin, the artillery was too much. Rifle clutched at arm's length, he sprang to his feet and began to clamber out of the trench. His comrades tried to grab him but he was too quick. Over the top of the trench he went, stumbling, scrambling, bellowing like a demented bull.

A one-man charge.

He hurled himself down the slope towards the Japs. A tiny, ridiculous figure, rifle pointed directly at the enemy, thrusting out from his waist, his legs blurring as they sped over the steep hill.

Down, down, down he went. For a moment it seemed that he might actually reach the Japs. Then there was a spattering of rifle fire from the valley. Baldwin tumbled and fell, his little body slithering along, his right arm reaching forward as if to grasp some prize.

Then he was on his feet again. He was turning around. Ridiculously, he was looking for his rifle. He couldn't find it. He fell to one knee, supporting himself on one hand. Another shot jarred him. He slipped silently to the ground and lay still.

The barrage continued until after dark. Then the Japanese infantry attacked again. The nightmarish illumination of flares revealed them as they scrambled forward, stumbling, firing at an enemy they couldn't see.

The attack petered out.

As dawn stole over the jungle the defenders opened aching eyes and heard the busy chirping of crickets and savoured the heavy scent of the bougainvillaea blossom. Dawns were a delight. But soon the sun rose and the air became saturated and men's limbs became leaden with fatigue and minds were benumbed with the bloodiness of it all. The place was a mess of shell-holes; only bits of the huts remained standing; the slope was covered with the bodies of men who had died trying to wrest it from the defenders.

Men had to be shaken awake. Watch had to be kept. It was no time to relax vigilance. Every man had to take his turn at watch. If the Japs attacked during his rest period, it was too bad, hard bloody cheese, tough bloody titty.

Cornish dreamt of a hill in England, a hill with uncommonly steep sides and a road winding to the top, a hill populated entirely by tired, bedraggled troops wearing filthy tropicals and busbies. Along the twisting paths and between rows of burning huts, walked the gallant major, cheering, inspiring his men to greater and greater effort. Man your positions to the end! We will win! We will hold this hill forever! And the men kept responding as they had been doing for longer than any of them could remember. They kept on smiling and reloading and aiming and firing. The hill had become their world. Nothing mattered that didn't happen on the hill. No one mattered who was not on the hill. The gallant major kept walking, always managing to find new ways to inspire and cheer. He was never still, never silent. And Cornish kept following him, fearful and faithful. The paths were endless; they curved and twisted their ways through glades and forests and they were lined by soldiers whose cracked lips kept smiling and whose bony fingers kept snapping in salute—but they creaked as they moved, like old wooden dolls. Aircraft, great black machines with enormous wings, kept hurtling over the hill, dropping great bundles to the defenders below. Ammunition, rifles, swagger-sticks: the contents of the bundles were always the same. And when one machine had dropped its bundle another would take its place, humming like a gargantuan sewing-machine. One more shower of bundles would come tumbling down to bounce and break and send bullets and rifles and swagger-sticks rolling around the place. The gallant major was overjoyed by the arrival of each new bundle. They would, he declared over and over and over again, enable the troops to hold the hill for ever. There would never be a force strong enough to dislodge them. It would be the greatest defence action in the history of warfare. It was something to celebrate. Brandy. Enamelled mugs. But Cornish waved his drink aside. Something had captured his attention on the slope. He asked Kerr for the binoculars. He adjusted the focus. Twiddle-twiddle. Now the picture was strong and sharp. Women: in brightly coloured skirts that swept the grass. Men: in morning suits. Wearing top hats. Strolling about the hill. Arm in arm, chatting, laughing, flirting. And stepping daintily over the bodies of men who had died trying to take the hill. No one looked down at the dead, waxen faces; no one looked up at the defenders with admiration. No one cared. No one gave a damn.

Cornish woke up. His neck hurt; he had been lying against a trench wall, half doubled up. He found Firmin beside him. And catastrophe was written in his eyes. Yet again.

'What is it?'

'Sir ... Major Kerr ... a mortar ...'

14

Mud? You didn't know what the stuff was unless you'd been at Passchendaele. Reclaimed marshland, that's all the whole stinking battlefield was. And the rain never stopped. People said it was because of the artillery; never had there been such weather, never in all the history of man on earth, they said. Rain turned the place into the biggest, hungriest, foulest-smelling bog in the world. It would swallow anything. It did. Men, tanks, horses, guns. Any bloody thing. A concrete pillbox went down one night. Vanished. With five men inside. Not a trace. You could get so caked in mud that you couldn't stand up, no matter how you tried; you were too bloody heavy for yourself. You swallowed mud by the ton. And the microbes and germs and assorted animal life that went with it. And you got trench tummy, dug-out diarrhœa, the Haig heaves, the Great-War-To-End-All-War shits. A man took a wrong step, off the duckboard, he was up to his waist in a flash. No chance of doing anything for him. It was too late. No use him screaming, nothing anyone could do; no one was strong enough to pull a man out of that filthy stuff.

So why couldn't Brian realize that and stop screaming?

Kerr awoke. Bellowing. And at once the pain almost flattened him. His consciousness reeled. He saw Brian. He saw Gibbs. He saw an orderly. Potter. Porter. Porson. No; not Porson. Oh God, had anything ever hurt quite so bloody cruelly? Someone was slicing his insides with a red-hot knife....

'Ah, you're awake.'

Gibbs.

He tried—oh, how he tried—to congratulate Gibbs on his perspicacity. But no words came.

Gibbs was leaning over him. Sweaty, unshaven face he had. Why the bloody hell hadn't Gibbs shaved? What the hell was everything coming to when an officer went around with a chin like a bloody beachcomber's?

'You caught one in the rear end, sir.'

Gasp. Croak. 'What?'

Thank Christ something came out.

'A chunk of mortar. It caught you in the buttock. It severed the gluteal artery but I've managed to stop the bleeding and clean things up. You'll be all right, sir.'

'You're bloody right I will....

A large motor-car. An enormous bonnet. Pointing down the High Street like the prow of a ship. Sun sparkling on the polished surface. The reflections of shabby houses, distorted as hell, skinny and tall one moment, squat and flat the next. Marvellous power under that bonnet. A touch on the accelerator: a prance forward like a bitch in heat. Pedestrians scattering. Alarm and respect in their cloddish faces.

Then. Absolutely not an instant's warning. There, directly in front of the angular grille: a pram. Black with yellow trim. Shining chrome-plated wheels. Crumpling, scattering wire spokes; wooden sides splitting; paint falling away in great flakes. Tiny voice squealing. Tiny hand raised in futile defence. Tiny eyes big with alarm. Tiny body flattened and torn by the great senseless monster ...

'Now take it easy, sir, take it easy.'

Hands were pressing down on his shoulders. An orderly. Gibbs. A dream. Thank Christ.

Now Cornish stood beside Gibbs and was hearing all

about the bloody gluteal artery and the muscles and the necessity of removing bits of mortar and cloth and sundry items from the major's arse ... some danger of hæmorrhaging ... some pain ... should be all right.

Bloody sneaky mortar. Now Kerr remembered it. Landed right behind him. He was lucky not to have been cut in half ... and he was lucky he hadn't been walking *towards* the bloody thing—what a loss to the women of Britain if it had caught him in the front!

God, but it hurt. It felt as if he was balanced on pain, like a ping-pong ball on a fountain, bouncing, bobbing, for anyone to take a pot-shot at.

He had to tell Cornish. It was imperative. Everything depended on Cornish understanding ...

'We must hold on,' he said—but it was little more than a husky whisper. At first it seemed it hadn't been heard; then Cornish's face was near, his eyes anxious.

'What was that, sir?'

'I said we must hold on. You understand?'

'Yes, sir. I understand.'

'There must be no thought of surrender.'

'No, sir.'

'I'm relying on you, Brian, er, Dave, lad.'

Cornish frowned briefly at the name, then he nodded.

'You'll soon be feeling better, sir.'

'We're holding this position, Dave.' He grasped Cornish's wrist. 'That's an order, d'you understand?'

Cornish was nodding as Kerr drifted back into unconsciousness.

Cornish took off his shirt and held it under the water of a stream. He splashed the water on his body; he soaked his head. His head still ached; now, however, it was a clean ache. That was some sort of an improvement.

From the slope came the occasional snap of a rifle shot. It was oddly muted, harmless-sounding. It wasn't enough to keep a man awake.

Cornish sat on the grass. His head throbbed and his eyes seemed about to snap out of focus. Fatigue lay on him like a heavy blanket, lined with tiny needles, one for every nerve.

Two shots, then another; the hint of an echo.

One must regard a situation with as much objectivity as one can muster, his father was fond of saying. The man who succeeds in business is the one who can view a situation with what might be termed a God-like eye. In other words, he thinks beyond the situation as it affects him personally at this precise point in time. Rather he thinks of its broad effects and its long-term effects. In military terms, he thinks strategically instead of tactically. When one has done that and when one has satisfied oneself that one is absolutely right, then one must determine a course of action and pursue it enthusiastically and, where necessary, ruthlessly, no matter what immediate side-effects that course of action might have.

'But, Father,' Cornish said, 'the difficulty here is that the course of action we are pursuing seems likely to get us all killed in the very near future. We are obeying orders with commendable devotion but our ammunition is dwindling rapidly and there seems to be no sign of any more on the way. It seems probable that we will die. And I don't want to. I suppose the truth of it is that I don't think this rotten hill is worth my life. To be honest, I don't think the entire Malaya Peninsula is worth it, but that's between us, Pater old boy.'

He discovered that he had been speaking aloud. Hurriedly he looked around. Thank God: no one was within earshot.

He stood up. The road led away to the south, to Singapore, to security. But undoubtedly it was lined with Japs only too eager for the British to use it. Ergo, the road had to be considered a dead loss. Which left the jungle—and one's chances were pretty grim in there.

Really, when you sat down and thought about it, there were only two courses of action: to fight or to surrender. If the fight was continued, the ammunition would soon be gone and then there would be no fight. Surrender? The Japs weren't known to be particularly well disposed toward prisoners. And they would probably like these British troops even less than the average.

Kerr had put his faith in reinforcements.

He refused to consider the possibility of defeat.

Which presumably made him a gallant officer.

Perhaps reinforcements and supplies *would* arrive, somehow or other. It was possible. It could accurately be described as a very real possibility.

Why then didn't the stupid bastards come?

From the remains of the *kongsi-house* he looked down on the hill's defenders. The Sodden Scarecrows. How would they vote if given the opportunity? Tick off one: Fight on; Surrender; Run Like Hell. He smiled wryly, conjuring up an election-like scene: himself and Kerr standing on ammunition boxes addressing the men, seeking support. It wasn't hard to guess who would win. Ah but it wasn't fair: Kerr had the gift of the gab, he looked good standing on ammo boxes, he could turn on charm at will....

Cornish sighed. The world would, he considered, be a far pleasanter place if no one possessed qualities of leadership....

The Japanese infantry filed out of the jungle and began to climb the hill yet again. Watchers observed an awesome sense of purpose in their movements. This time, each step seemed to say, we will reach the top of the hill and drive the British off. This time we will not be stopped.

Soberly the Tommies regarded their enemy's approach. Men glanced meaningfully at their neighbours as if taking a look while it was still possible. Then their eyes returned to the slope. Every bloody Jap in Malaya seemed to be coming up it.

Hell's bloody bells, Cornish thought numbly.

Row after row appeared, their helmets bobbing like a metallic sea. There were twice as many of them ... impossible to stop them ... foolish even to try....

That's enough! He had to shout the order to himself. For Christ's sake, pull yourself together! A commander should always regard a situation positively; his attitude and demeanour will inevitably influence those around him, etcetera, etcetera....

He walked behind the crouched soldiers with their levelled rifles and their heads angled as they peered through fore and aft sights. His innards churned in apprehension. Should he bring in the men from the other faces? No, not yet; the Japs might try a flanking movement. Later on, perhaps, it might be wise ... if there was a later on ... if there were any men to bring.

A Scots soldier glanced at him as he walked past. He had a young face but his mouth and eyes were far too old.

Milne, revolver in hand, said, 'A big party this time, David.'

'I suppose we should feel flattered.'

'We'll cope,' said Milne.

'Rather,' said Cornish.

The Japanese plodded on, their bodies angled to take the incline. They looked down at the ground as they walked, with only occasional glances at the positions they had to take.

And why did you desert in the face of the enemy?
It seemed the only intelligent thing to do.
'How's Major Kerr, sir?'
'He'll be all right, you can rest assured of that.'
'Thank you, sir.'

There was no longer any need to tell the British troops when to open fire. They all knew to a yard or two how far the Japs were permitted to come. And so they waited, their muscles bracing for the impact of the first recoil. Almost there. Time to start picking individual targets. Time to play God.

Scores of fingers squeezed scores of triggers at almost the same instant. It sounded like one shot, in component parts, continuous yet subtly broken. The Brens opened up, sending short, vicious bursts of half a dozen rounds into the advancing men. The advance was shaken; the leading men crumpled and fell. The stink of cordite swept back on the British troops.

God, I wish we had a Bren for every man, thought Cornish. It would be marvellous; we could slaughter men so much more efficiently. Marvellous, he thought, marvellous.

So numerous were the attackers that they found it difficult to side-step a casualty as his body tumbled and rolled back down the hill. The British troops laughed outright when one dead Jap bowled over half a dozen of his comrades, his lifeless body catching them at ankle level as it slithered backwards.

Then, after a brief chuckle, it was back to the serious business of killing. Target nicely lined up: aim for the body just above the stomach: less chance of missing. Gentle, completely professional squeeze of the trigger. Bang. Down goes another Nip.

The Japanese return fire was methodical and accurate.

A rifleman fell at Cornish's feet. A bullet had hit him in the centre of the forehead.

Cornish dropped to one knee. There was nothing to be done for the man. He took the rifle; its stock was still warm from living hands. The dead man had been on the point of pulling the trigger. Cornish raised it, felt the unfamiliar weight of it against his shoulder, felt the tremor of his hands against it. He hadn't fired a rifle since OCTU. There, the shooting had been done on a field with targets at one end, a trench immediately before them, in which men crouched holding sticks with small discs at the end. The discs were held over the bullet holes to tell the marksmen how accurate they had been.

Cornish aimed at a squat, ugly-looking fellow, an officer by the look of him. Bang. The rifle kicked, jarring him. Damn. The ugly-looking officer kept coming. Cornish grabbed for the bolt. It felt awkward. Up and back, then a good thrust forward against the spring to shove the next round up from the magazine into the breech; finally, a swift downward movement to lock it. He closed one eye and squinted along the barrel. His finger shook slightly as he pressed the trigger. Down went the ugly-looking Jap, hands clutching at air.

Shot, sir, said Cornish to himself. He felt triumph touching the corners of his lips. His hand was no longer trembling. Just kill enough people and you won't be frightened, he thought.

He fired again. Missed. And again.

Around him, the gunfire was a continuous roar, no longer a series of separate detonations. The din assaulted the ears like an endless drum-roll.

The rifle became stingingly hot in Cornish's hands as he fired shot after shot at the foreign men with sweating, anxious faces. The foreign men fell ... but there were always more ... they kept coming, a tide of humanity.

Cornish put the rifle down.

'Keep it up, men,' he yelled but his voice was a squeak in that din.

He scrambled to his feet. Oh God, how near the Japs were ... and how numerous. Was it time to throw in every last man? Yes, he decided rapidly; it was now or never. Everyone had to be brought in, every man capable of holding a rifle. He ordered the last logs cut free. They bounced down the hill, knocking men down, dulling the impetus of the advance for a few moments. But the logs were forgotten at once as new drives were organized. Obediently, enthusiastically it seemed, the Japanese troops pushed forward. Their goal lay only a few dozen yards away. This time they would reach it—for the glory of the Emperor and the sacred destiny of Japan.

Cornish ran across the road and on to the higher ground. He could see almost the entire line, and the enemy. He knew he was exposing himself to any one of God knows how many riflemen, but he had to see the whole picture....

We can't stop them this time, he thought; it's impossible. Panic boiled within him. In a moment the Japs would reach the British positions and it would be man against man, bayonets and *parangs* slashing through bone and muscle. Blood splashing everywhere, drenching, staining....

No—for Christ's sake get a hold of yourself! Now! This instant! Cornish stared, forcing his brain to think and apply logic to what his eyes saw. Is there anything, he asked himself, anything I can do to prevent this? Think! Think!

He gave orders for the last men on the east and west faces to be brought forward.

An ammo supplier was hit; he lay on the road quite still, his mouth wide open. Cornish ran to him, took his load of cartridges and passed them rapidly to the riflemen. No time to worry about whether the poor fellow was alive or dead.

'I'm not at all sure we can hold them,' Milne shouted, his face grey and strained.

'Of course we can! Don't be so bloody silly!'

Cornish ran on before Milne had time to respond. He didn't want to hear Milne's response; there was nothing to be gained from it, nothing to be learnt. He stopped and fired his revolver six times at the enemy without apparent effect. Behind him, a grenade burst with a dull, hollow bang. He felt the slap of blast on his back. Somewhere on his left a man bellowed in pain.

He crouched behind a log and reloaded his revolver. Head up, cautiously. The Japs were pouring up the hill ... and so bloody *many* of them. He aimed. The gun bucked in his hand as he pulled the trigger. Second shot, third ... yes, a man fell. Fourth shot, fifth, sixth. A bullet whined past his head. His skin contracted momentarily. A close one, he thought, too busy to react. He thrust more bullets into the warm cylinder. Left arm up, bent back as if to look at your watch; instead place revolver on it, use it as a steadying platform ...

He fired at them but still they came.

'More ammo!' someone yelled. 'For fuck's sake, bring us some more ammo!'

Then a Japanese private, in shorts and an open-necked shirt appeared, scrambling on to the breastwork, only a few yards from Cornish. His breathing was loud and laboured. *Audible.* Cornish raised his revolver. He pulled the trigger.

Nothing happened. He hadn't reloaded.

Faintly surprised, the Jap pulled himself over the barricade, bringing both hands to bear on his rifle as he did so.

At the same instant, Cornish saw a Lee Enfield on the ground a couple of yards away—it must have been dropped there by a man wounded or killed. As he hurled himself down to grab it, he heard the shot and felt the bullet sizzling past him and thudding into the ground. His fingers clutched the British weapon, closed around its smooth stock.

The Jap fired again.

His bullet caught the epaulette on Cornish's shirt, neatly removing the button.

Cornish reeled, almost fell. For an awful fragment of time he believed himself shot. But still he pulled at the weight of the rifle, dragging it away from the mud. The Jap had already pulled his bolt back, to ready himself for the next shot. He was fast but he was expending precious instants. Cornish wondered whether the man who owned the rifle had cocked it before he dropped it. If he didn't, Cornish thought, the Jap will be able to fire before I will.

He didn't take aim; he simply slapped the weapon against his right hip and pulled the trigger.

Lucky. Oh God, how lucky. The rifle fired. And the bullet caught the Jap fair and square in the middle of the stomach. He folded up, his jaw dropping.

Cornish took careful aim and shot the man through the head. He noticed as he fired that the man's eyes were tightly shut.

The epaulette slopped on his shoulder, memento of a distinctly close thing.

'Nice shooting, sir,' said someone or other.

No time to look at the speaker. No time to wonder at the closeness of the escape. No time to do anything but fire and keep firing into the surging lines of infantry.

But—oh God—it was useless to try and stop them. There were too many of them; no matter how many you shot down more kept coming, shimmering bayonets held before them. In a little while it would all be over.

It was then that Kerr appeared.

Cornish stared. He was seeing things. Kerr couldn't be

there because he was wounded and flat on his back and ...

But Kerr was there. And he was walking. True, he leant heavily on a stick but he was managing it on his own, although McGregor was near at hand, a sodden study in devotion.

'Sir? What the hell are you doing?'

Pain seemed to blur Kerr's features. But he smiled and clamped the empty Dunhill between his teeth. He wore his trousers and shirt but was bareheaded.

'Couldn't sleep for all the noise you bastards were making.'

A man laughed.

And Kerr limped over to the first trench.

Within moments every man on the hill knew that Kerr was back in action. And a change came over them. Something happened to them. If Mad Old Ernie was able to get up and strut around, there was still hope. Lots of hope. Mad Old Ernie. The Japs weren't much good if they couldn't get him down. And they couldn't. There he was: proof, walking proof that in spite of their suicidal efforts, the Japs had won precisely nothing. A great voice, a jutting pipe, a superbly unafraid human being ... and he was laughing and mocking the Japs and asking one's private opinion on the most efficient way of putting paid to the little bastards and asking if one would mind greatly if he had a go with one's rifle....

And because of him, men snapped their triggers a fraction of an instant faster and faced the enemy with a fraction less fear. Will itself became a weapon. The will of the British troops increased just as the will of the Japanese troops decreased because they had driven themselves to the limit. The Japanese had no Major Kerr to dole out confidence in great booming doses. Their pressure slackened just as they came closest to victory. They fell to cover, scrambling behind comrades' bodies, hugging the indifferent ground. They still fired but their fierce determination had evaporated and had blown away. Frantically their officers and N.C.O.s ran among them, trying to rally them, striking with canes, slapping with open hands. Some men did obey and tried to renew the advance. But they were easy targets, cut down at once. The spirit, the *élan* had gone. Painfully, shamed, the Japanese slipped back down the hill.

At the top of the hill, Kerr stood, hands on his hips.

'I told you!' he yelled at his men. 'You didn't believe me, but I told you you were better than them! Now do you believe me? Do you?'

Yes, they believed him now! They grinned and laughed at him. They believed anything he cared to tell them.

Kerr had to be carried back to his bunk. He kept gasping out his thanks. Everyone was being so kind but it wasn't necessary; he could manage....

'Careful with his legs.'

'Yes, sir.' With infinite tenderness, McGregor lifted Kerr's legs on to the bunk.

Cornish told him to go and get the M.O. at the double.

Kerr's eyes were closed. Cornish thought he had fainted. Carefully he unbuttoned the major's shirt. Even prostrate, wounded, the man managed to look trim, a credit to the military profession. Hair neatly trimmed—did McGregor cut it? Crisply shaved—not stubbly chinned like every other man on the hill. Fingernails brushed clean—God, had the man brought a nail-brush *here*?

Cornish sighed. He supposed that it simplified things when one's life consisted of a single journey, so to speak. Aim for one goal, not a hundred. Perhaps that was the secret of the whole miserable business. Regimentation, simplification, organization. Kerr was a happy man because of it. No side-issues for our Ernie. He knew precisely what he had to do and why at any given moment. So did Tom Byrne. It was all spelled out. Just follow the simple directions and you need have no fears, you will know you are doing The Right Thing.

'Dave, lad ...'

Kerr was smiling weakly.

'How are you feeling, sir?'

'Champion ... it only smarts a bit.' He nodded. 'You did well, Dave, you pushed them back ...'

'You turned up in the nick of time, sir.'

Kerr's face was white beneath its tan; sweat streamed across his brow. 'They can't beat us, Dave. They've tried everything. They still can't beat us. We're going to hold this hill, Dave....'

'Yes, but the ammo....'

'We'll hold on, Dave, d'you understand.' His voice was suddenly firm. His eyes bored into Cornish's.

'Yes, sir, but ...'

'It's an order.'

15

Cornish slept fitfully, like a man with a fever. He awoke several times during the night and wondered whether he was coming down with some dread tropical disease. Or perhaps measles. He had never had measles. In the morning he was woken by the sun. Already the hill was steaming like a sweating horse. He ate a few dry biscuits and drank some water. His stomach ached.

Tom Byrne was saying Mass nearby, intoning the sacred words to a dozen men kneeling bareheaded before him.

Blessed are they, thought Cornish sourly, who slaughter their fellow men with devotion and efficiency.

He stood up, wobbled a little, and began to walk along the road to where Milne was talking to Johnson in his brisk and urgent way.

There was a huge hole in the middle of the road. It was half full of dirty water. Cornish paused to look at it. He smiled. There was something marvellously obstinate about life. An ingeniously designed high explosive device blows a poor fellow to bits and, in the process, creates a hole in the road. Then it rains. The hole fills up. Life promptly starts all over again. The amoeba becomes the water-bug which in turn becomes the tadpole or something which wriggles its way on to dry land and eventually works its way up to become man. Or perhaps it's a case of working its way down, Cornish thought. The shell giveth life and the shell taketh life away. A few lines for Tom to add to his routine.

He frowned. Something had occurred to him. It was

quiet. He hadn't heard a shot since he awoke. And now, only the voices of men and the burbling of animals and the gentle murmur of wind were to be heard.

He walked over to Milne.

'Peaceful, what?' Milne's lower face smiled.

'What's the story?'

'Don't know, old boy. Can't understand it.'

Cornish stepped forward, on to the slippery ledge. There was nothing to see but a scattering of Japanese corpses, puffed and foul, some weapons and equipment.

'Their vehicles are still there. See them? On the road.'

'Yes, I see them,' said Cornish. He felt a stupid stab of disappointment. The Japs hadn't packed up and left.

'There hasn't been a peep out of them since dawn.'

'Perhaps it's a Japanese holiday; the Emperor's birthday or something.'

Unexpectedly, Milne burst into laughter. 'That's jolly funny, David, jolly funny.'

Cornish didn't think so. His stomach heaved. Those bloody biscuits.

Around them, men were cautiously emerging from their trenches, looking in every direction like animals checking all approaches before leaving their lair.

Had the Jap commander asked his air-force chums for another raid? Cornish looked, but the sky seemed innocent. Even the clouds were now dispersing as if to show that they had nothing to hide. There was no sound of motors. Startled, he turned as a large bird flapped its wings, struggling to find lift in the humid air to take it up from the jungle.

The sun rose higher in a sky of coppery-blue. The wind gathered strength and fluttered the shirt-sleeves of the dead Japs on the slope and stirred the tall trees. The British troops relaxed. One man stood beside his trench and proceeded to touch his toes fifty times, revelling in the opportunity to exercise. Another undid his shorts and urinated down the slope toward the enemy. Someone cautioned him: a sniper might take aim and shoot it off. Someone else said that even a crack Jap sniper couldn't hit a target that small. Many men slept. Others took their clothes off and washed them. Some men shaved, hacking at the growth of days, frowning as they found faces not quite as they were remembered. They were thinner; that was to be expected; but there was an odd angularity about the features, a set to the mouth and a look in the eyes that didn't quite seem to belong. The men's bodies were incredibly filthy. Sweat and dirt had combined to form a greasy film that required peeling as much as washing off. It was an effort; but it had to be admitted that feeling clean was quite splendid. Some men wandered from their trenches. They didn't go far. There was nowhere to go. The village was a sorry mess, just a pile of matchwood, most of it burnt to ashes. Shell-holes were everywhere. And if you looked too closely you would find hands or legs or parts that couldn't be identified. And so men wandered back to their trenches and awaited their enemy's pleasure.

As he entered, Gibbs raised his eyebrows. 'I quite expected to find you dead,' he said cheerfully—'sir.'

'Bugger off,' said Kerr. 'Never felt better.'

In fact, he had never felt worse. Pain throbbed through him with a maddening, corrosive regularity. He had cursed the pain all night, absorbing its attacks and telling it he could hardly feel it, accusing it of weakening, losing its power. With the dawn and the coolness and the freshness of the hour before the sun rose high, he had thought the worst over. But as the heat of the day increased so did the intensity of the pain.

Gibbs smiled. 'I quite thought you'd hæmorrhage fatally when you went for that silly stroll of yours.'

'Disappointed, were you?'

'No, amazed.' Gibbs started to remove the dressings. 'You must have the constitution of a water buffalo.'

Kerr winced, but doggedly shook his head when Gibbs asked him if he was in pain. 'Bloody terrible bedside manner you've got.'

'Please don't hesitate to call another man in, sir.'

'You're all as bad as each other.'

Oh Christ but it hurt. His vision blurred. Who would guess the bloody buttocks could hurt so much? Gibbs was saying something to McGregor. Telling him not to let Major Kerr get up under any circumstances whatsoever. Telling him to keep Major Kerr quiet. Lots of rest. Bunches of grapes. Flowers. Boxes of chocolates. Funny little wool jacket, white, fluffy. Son and heir held up for inspection. Bags of pride. Nipper as ugly as hell. Like all new-born nippers. Lots of foolish talk about his eyes and chin. Hard enough to spot any resemblance between him and a human being, let alone between mother or father....

Everything had been so incredibly perfect. It was as if fate had let him do the planning for a change. He had applied for a permanent commission. Much to his astonishment, he was awarded one. Then he thought about it. Why should he be so astonished? Hadn't he volunteered *before* the outbreak of war? And wasn't he now an officer *and* a colonel's son-in-law? Indeed he had and indeed he was. He thanked every German gunner for missing him and, slightly ashamed but quite sincerely, he thanked God and Kaiser Wilhelm for sending that war at that particular time. If it hadn't been for the two of them, he would probably be doffing cotton in Rochdale now instead of being saluted and admired.

'What are you thinking about?'
'I'm wondering how long it will take me to become a field marshal.'
'When I was ten I swore I would never, under any circumstances, marry a soldier.'
'Are you glad you did?'
'No. You're a disgusting man, like all soldiers. You always have your hand on my breasts or up my legs.'
'Lucky girl. There's many a lass would be only too happy to have a slap and tickle from me.'
'Conceited oaf.'
'I'm just stating the truth.'
'All soldiers are inveterate liars. My mother told me that. Now I believe her.'
'All you have to do is ask. I'll resign my commission and take employment as a car salesman or a commercial traveller or possibly an inspector of gas meters.'
'The trouble is, you look so handsome in your uniform.'
'I understand that a gas inspector is issued with quite a natty uniform.'
'We mustn't let our marriage go flat and stale. We must promise always to be as happy as we are today.'
'Aye. I promise.'
'It's adorable, the way you say "Aye".'
'I have a feeling your mother and the colonel don't think it's adorable.'
'Well, you do take a bit of getting used to, you know.'
'Getting used to?'
'Yes; you're quite direct. Anyway, Mummy and Daddy are learning to love you just as I do.'
'Not quite as you do, I hope. Your mother is a charming woman but I don't fancy her in bed; and as for the colonel ...'
'I didn't mean that. You have a filthy mind.'

'It's part of my charm.'
'Yes, you do have charm. Dangerous.'
'Dangerous?'
'I keep thinking of hot nights in the tropics.'
'Why?'
'You might be sent to the tropics. And the tropics do something to the blood. In India, frightfully well-brought-up people are forever exchanging wives and husbands. Daddy has a story about a brigadier who was found in bed with the sixteen-year-old daughter of a sergeant-major. It's something to do with the heat and the humidity, I believe. You get so randy, you don't care who you do it with.'
'I only want to do it with you.'
'That's good, because if you ever do it with anyone else I shall ... cut it off—with my nail scissors.'
'In that case, love, you can be sure of one thing.'
'What's that?'
'I'll never tell.'

It was foggy the day Brian was born. And it was a hellish, maddening job to get to the nursing-home. He had to sit in a taxi that crawled at little more than walking pace. His nervous hands dismembered a perfectly good pair of gloves. His mouth was dry and sour from too many cigarettes. Finally he arrived, hot and frantic with fear of what ghastly, unspeakable things must have happened while the taxi dawdled. But the receptionist was quite calm; oh, dear no; it wasn't over yet, not by a long chalk. Would Mr Kerr have a seat, please?

One hundred and ninety-seven minutes later he was a father. A son, it was announced. A hearty eight-and-a-half-pounder. Mother doing splendidly, thank you very much.

In the months that followed he had consumed happiness in great draughts, absorbing it lustily, unthinkingly, for it seemed that there would always be more. Happiness was surely his due, his just reward for valiant services rendered, his prize for charm and good looks and daring and a way with colonels' daughters. He rented a small white house with a grey front door and roof, in Royston, near Cambridge.

The days of peace seemed full of promise.

Then, one day in June, Colonel Hatton died. Quite suddenly. Quite painlessly. He simply ceased living. Louise was distraught. For three days she sobbed out her misery. Kerr began to to be afraid she might literally die of a broken heart. He gave her some brandy. She refused; she hated the stuff. He insisted. She drank it; it warmed her; she had more. Kerr was obliged to leave on a gunnery course. He took his wife and son to the late colonel's house in London and left for Catterick. Five days later, Louise's mother telephoned him and told him there had been an accident. Brian was hurt. Terribly. In fact...

At first Kerr's brain refused to accept it. He hung up the receiver and stared at it. He was confused and disoriented, as if he had been struck hard in the face. Had he actually heard those words? No, for God's sake, he must have imagined the whole thing. It was beyond the realm of possibility, far beyond....

Someone—he could never recall who—drove him to the railway station. In a kind of trance he bought his ticket and boarded a train south. He sat and watched the countryside, bright with new life. Inexorably the truth implanted itself. It was foolish to hope, foolish to believe that Mrs Hatton might have had her facts hopelessly wrong, that the whole thing was a monstrous mistake, that Brian was alive....

Louise was terrifyingly calm. As he opened the front door, she said, 'Brian is dead. There's nothing you can do.'

She spoke loudly, harshly, as if to squash any arguments

before they were uttered. Her face was deathly pale and her skin had a taut look that accentuated the set of her cheekbones. She held herself unusually erect. Kerr realized with a pang that she had never looked lovelier. Then, in an almost physical way, he felt his own sense of loss overshadowed by compassion for her. He wanted to hold her, protect her from a fate which had suddenly become so vindictive. When she turned abruptly and walked up the stairs, he started to follow. Then he stopped; she was shaking her head in a tiny but unmistakable motion. He stood in the hallway and watched her go into the bedroom. The key turned. He found himself staring through the open drawing-room door. One of Brian's toys, a golliwog, sat primly in the corner of the settee, an inane smile on its black face. Tears blurring his vision, Kerr took the toy and held it. Jesus Christ, Brian must have been playing with the thing only hours before; it was still slightly sticky to the touch. In an agony of helplessness, he clutched the golliwog to his chest. He cried for half an hour and then he had no tears left.

Louise stayed in the bedroom until the next day. When she emerged, she was drunk. Messily drunk. She had embarked on a lifelong career.

Soon Kerr was mourning his wife just as he mourned his son. He had lost both of them. Louise's surrender to alcohol was absolute. And when she was capable of speech it was vitriolic. She hated him and she was adamant that he stay away from her. Her skin crawled, she managed to inform him, at the thought of him touching her. He was a beastly common pig; she detested him; she didn't know how he had persuaded her to marry him.... He tried to talk to her; he was alternately gentle and firm. But the effort was wasted; she had found her sanctum in the brandy bottle.

Various M.O.s and padres were sympathetic but could

offer little practical assistance. There were vague references to places where people went for 'cures' but, he was told, the patient had to 'have the will'. Soon Kerr learnt to accept the fact that his wife was a hopeless alcoholic.

Simultaneously, his career seemed to come to a standstill. He discovered to his dismay that the peacetime army bore little resemblance to its wartime counterpart. The army without a war was a club—and its membership was almost static. It did not expand to create opportunities for ambitious young officers; indeed there seemed every prospect of it diminishing in size as the years marched by. Kerr was just one of many who had to wait for older officers to retire or die. There was no point in hoping for Accelerated Promotion. Accelerated Promotion went only to well-spoken young gentlemen who had been to the right schools and who had well-placed relatives and whose wives were bright, decorative creatures who knew when to smile and what to say and how much to drink. No Accelerated Promotion for Lieutenant E. G. Kerr aged 25, 30, 35, 36, 37, 38.... Was he the oldest lieutenant in the British army? He found himself making enquiries about other men's ages. Soon they would retire him. And what then? No handsomely-salaried executive positions awaited middle-aged lieutenants with Lancashire accents and sots for wives....

Then four of Hitler's brigades marched into the Rhineland.

McGregor appeared, panting damply.
'Are you awake, sir?'
'My eyes are open, laddie.'
'Aye, sir, sorry sir. Mr Cornish told me to tell you—'
'Tell me what?'
'There's something going on, sir. They've got a flag.'
'A what?'

'A flag, sir. A white flag.'

It appeared behind the trees. You could see it moving about, like a fluttering bird trying to find its way out.

Then it emerged.

It was a white flag. A soldier held it. Behind him were five more soldiers.

The British troops glanced at one another. Their eyes asked one another what to make of this. A white flag? The Japs?

Rifle-bolts clicked.

'No shooting,' Cornish shouted, surprised at the loudness of his voice. 'Pass the word along, quickly. Keep them covered but don't shoot.'

The Japs were walking up the road. Six diminutive figures: the flag looked like a sail that was blowing them along.

Cornish rubbed his eyes. The Japs picked their way past the bodies of their comrades: and never a glance down at the poor bastards.

To the left a rifle barrel angled down at the Japs.

'"No shooting," I said.'

One of the Japanese glanced up towards the British. Had he heard the shout? Had his heart pounded, thinking it was an order to open fire?

The two men immediately behind the flag-carrier were officers. Squat fellows in breeches and open-necked shirts, they wore soft caps and swords around their waists. They're too damned short for swords, Cornish thought. What if one of them trips and falls flat on his face? Would the disgrace mean ceremonial suicide, *hara-kiri*?

'Ugly buggers.'

Cornish nodded without looking to see who had spoken. What the hell were the Japs up to? He felt slightly sick. He gave orders for everyone to keep an extra-special watch on the hill's other faces.

'If they're comin' for lunch, they got a bleedin' disappointment in store.'

'I could get that bastard right in the balls.'

'No shooting.'

'I was just thinking, sir.'

Now it was possible to hear the sound of the Japs' boots on the loose surface of the road. Trudge, trudge: even steps.

The Japs made their way around the remains of the tank.

Cornish suddenly wished he had a clean and well-pressed uniform; these rags were dismal things in which to meet one's enemy.

The Japs stopped twenty yards from the British positions. The men wore green tunics and khaki trousers.

The two officers took half a dozen paces forward, then unbuckled their swords and handed them back to aides.

Cornish glanced to the left and right. No one seemed about to shoot. He stood up.

The Japanese officers halted, saluted, inclined their heads and bowed jerkily.

The shorter of the two said, in good English, 'Good day, I bring you greetings from the Imperial Japanese Army.'

Greetings? Cornish wanted to laugh. How bloody absurd to talk about greetings. The Japs are as mad as us, he thought.

'Good afternoon,' he said.

Sweat glistened on the Japanese officer's flat-featured face. He looked about thirty. His eyes shifted from Cornish to the British troops and back again. His heavy breathing was clearly audible.

He's nervous, Cornish thought. And I don't blame him. I am too; I wish they'd shoot; I know what they're up to when they're shooting.

'I bring a message from my commanding officer to your commanding officer. I hoped that I might have the honour to address your commanding officer.'

Cornish nodded. 'He is ... in his quarters.'

He turned towards the cave. He found Kerr in view; McGregor had dragged his makeshift bunk to the entrance.

'Bring the buggers over here!'

The troops laughed. Good old Ernie.

Cornish said, 'Will you kindly follow me.'

They walked past the British soldiers with their thin arms folded and their lips proud and obstinate, around a shell hole in the middle of the road, boots thudding noisily in a world suddenly quiet.

Kerr, pale but bright-eyed, greeted the visitors. His hair was neatly brushed. McGregor must have shaved him; on his left cheek was a small nick, a fresh one.

'You wanted to see me, gentlemen? Well, here I am.'

'Good day, sir,'

'Aye, well, we'll see, won't we?'

'I beg your pardon, sir?'

'Never mind. It wasn't very funny.'

'I see, sir,' said the Japanese officer, who clearly didn't.

'What can I do for you?'

'Sir, I am Captain Watanabe. This is Lieutenant Fukui who accompanies me—'

'On what?'

'Sir?'

'Never mind. That wasn't very funny, either.'

In a large semi-circle about the cave entrance, the British soldiers were standing and sitting, relaxing, savouring the spectacle, sizing up the Japs, enjoying their discomfiture.

Watanabe continued, 'Sir, it is the wish of my commanding officer, Colonel Hoshi, and the wish of Lieutenant-

General Tomoyuki Yamashita, commanding officer of the 25th Army, that further bloodshed be avoided.'

Kerr shrugged. 'It's all right with me, lad.'

'There is, after all, little point in continuing the struggle now—'

'Aye, well, I think you put up a good fight. What d'you say, Dave?'

Cornish grinned in spite of himself.

Watanabe said hastily, 'Sir, I did not mean that *we*—'

'What did you mean, then?'

But Watanabe had lost his place in his by-the-heart speech; he had stumbled; now he had to pick up the pieces.

Cornish felt almost sorry for him.

'Sir, we come to address you as officers of the Imperial Japanese Army, full of respect for the courage and fortitude of your men. But we must ask—' he took a deep breath— 'that you lay down your arms.'

A few paces away, Milne frowned at the very suggestion.

'You what?' said Kerr mildly.

'Lay down your arms, sir.'

'Why should we?'

'Isn't it ... obvious, sir?'

'No.'

'Sir, surely you can see that there is now nothing to be gained by further resistance.'

'Really? You speak English well.'

Watanabe was taken aback. 'Sir?'

'Where did you learn it?'

'I was at Cambridge, sir, for some years, and at Cornell, in the United States.'

'I was at Cambridge, too,' said Kerr. 'In the barracks.'

'Sir, please excuse me for one minute.' With a tiny bow, Watanabe turned and talked quietly to Fukui.

Kerr seemed to be enjoying himself; he sucked on his

empty pipe with the air of a man who has all the time in the world.

The Japanese officers nodded and drew apart. Watanabe said, 'Sir, I must conclude that you are not aware of what has happened.'

'And what's that?'

'Sir, it is my duty to inform you that at eight o'clock on the morning of the 15th of February, General Yamashita accepted the surrender of Singapore from General Percival.'

No one said anything for a moment. Outside, an animal shrilled; the British riflemen still watched in stony silence, not hearing, therefore not reacting.

'That's a bloody lie,' said Kerr.

'No, it is the truth, sir.'

It must be a lie, Cornish said to himself. It must be a lie, an outrageous, unspeakable lie.

Kerr snapped, 'Don't waste my time with such bullshit, Captain!' His face darkened; a vein in his forehead stood out like an angry signal.

Watanabe blinked nervously. 'Sir,' he said, 'it is true. I swear it. And in view of the fact that Singapore has fallen, continued resistance is purposeless.' His pace quickened as if he feared being silenced before delivering his message. 'Your fight has been honourable and courageous but it is senseless to let more of your brave men die.'

Kerr said, 'Is that what you came all the way up here to tell me?'

'Yes, sir, that is the message I had the honour to bring.'

Kerr looked at him pityingly. 'Aye, well, here's a message you can have the honour of taking back to Colonel Whatever-His-Name-Is. Tell him, with my compliments, that I'm a bit too bloody old in the tooth for fairy stories.'

Watanabe looked puzzled. 'Sir? Your tooth? I do not understand. I am sorry.'

Kerr said, 'I am too old to believe in children's stories. Do you understand that?'

'Sir, it is not, I respectfully declare, a children's story.'

'Good day, Captain.'

'Sir, I deeply regret—'

'Aye, I regret all sorts of things too, Captain.' Kerr looked away rudely.

Watanabe took a deep breath. Awkwardly he said to Cornish. 'Please convey my thanks to your commanding officer. It was most kind of him to give so much of his valuable time.'

For an instant, Cornish thought the Japanese was being sarcastic. But no, it was just elaborate courtesy.

'Very well,' he said.

Watanabe said, 'And please ask him to believe what I have said about Singapore. It is true. I declare it on my honour as a Japanese officer—'

Kerr chuckled quietly and sniffed.

Watanabe flushed. 'I have been instructed to inform you that we will hold our fire for two hours while—' he groped for the foreign words—'while you consider the proposition.'

'I understand.'

'It is now five minutes before one o'clock. We will hold our fire until three o'clock if we have not heard—'

Without turning, Kerr interjected: 'That's two hours and five minutes, Captain. No favours, thank you very much. Two hours will bring us up to five minutes to three.'

'Very well, sir. Five minutes to three. Thank you. Good afternoon.'

The British troops had a final laugh when the Japanese party set off down the road. The Jap soldiers about-turned like two-legged tops, swinging themselves around in a single movement instead of using three steps on-the-spot as the good Lord intended it to be done.

16

At vast expense, fifteen-inch guns had been installed to protect Singapore; enormous weapons, they could hurl one-ton shells as far as twenty miles.
But only out to sea.
The best British experts had declared it inconceivable that any enemy would attempt an invasion of the island other than from the sea—despite the existence of some 1,000 miles of coastline on the peninsula. Meanwhile other experts, Japanese experts, had surveyed the situation and declared that as few as three divisions might accomplish the task of invading Malaya and subsequently taking Singapore.

The breeze had died and the heat, sodden and enervating, had descended on the hill. Men sat and sweated and waited. Those with a will to discuss such matters agreed to a man that at that particular time and place they would much rather have a cool pint of bitter or nut brown ale or Guinness than Paulette Goddard.
Half an hour to go.
Cornish had been busy inspecting the positions, discussing ammunition—and thinking about Watanabe.
Kerr was asleep; orders had been issued that he was to be awakened ten minutes before the end of the cease-fire.
It seemed quiet in the valley. But God knew what the trees concealed. More reinforcements, more artillery? Were the troops at this very moment being told that failure would not be tolerated under any circumstances? Was some officer,

stung by H.Q. rebukes, telling them that the hill had to be taken, no matter what the cost? Perhaps Watanabe was tightening the chin-strap of his steel helmet in preparation for combat. An odd feeling, knowing one of them, no matter how slightly. Watanabe spoke English well, faithfully enunciating every syllable. Had he enjoyed his time at Cambridge? Had the English students treated him well? Did he think kindly of them? Ah, but what the hell did it matter what he thought?

Milne was rocking back and forth on his heels like an athlete waiting for the next event.

'Won't be too long now, old boy.'

Shut up, for Christ's sake, Cornish thought but didn't say. His stomach hurt. Was it funk? Or indigestion? Or both?

Milne said what a lot of cock the Jap had talked about Singapore. Cornish nodded. Then a thought occurred to him. It was a chilling thought. He prodded it mentally, examined it from every angle. God, it seemed sound; frighteningly so.

'I'm going to see Major Kerr,' he said.

He found him on his feet, leaning on the chair while McGregor fastened a webbing belt around his waist.

'Good God, sir, what are you doing up?'

Kerr smiled, not easily. 'Couldn't lie around any longer. Waiting is a pain in the arse, isn't it? Literally, in my case.'

'But you shouldn't be up. Mike Gibbs said—'

'Bugger Mike Gibbs. He's an old woman. What's the time?'

'It's ten to three.'

'Fourteen-fifty hours, you mean, don't you?' said Kerr, grinning. 'Time we went out. The fun'll be starting in a little while. Don't want to miss it. You buzz off,' he told

McGregor. 'Captain Cornish can give me a hand outside.'

McGregor saluted and scurried away.

'But sir—' Cornish began to protest Kerr's getting up.

Kerr snapped, 'I'm not going to lie down now, Dave lad, and that's final.'

Cornish shrugged and nodded, numbed by the realization that Kerr thought this would be the final battle and that he would probably die.

Kerr's breathing was loud and painful as he attempted to stand upright alone. 'No damn ... I'll have to use the bloody stick.'

Cornish said, 'Sir, there's something I have to talk to you about.'

Kerr chuckled, the sweat pouring from him. 'Yes, lad, you have my permission to marry.'

'Marry?'

'A joke, for Christ's sake.'

'Sorry, sir.'

'You don't laugh enough, that's your trouble, Dave; you're a sober-sided bastard, for a young lad.'

Cornish plunged. 'Sir, is there any way the Japs could know that we're out of touch with our main forces?'

'Uh? I don't know; no, I shouldn't think so.'

'Don't you see—the Japs were *surprised* that we didn't know about Singapore falling.'

'Singapore hasn't fallen!'

'I think it has, sir. The Japs *assumed* we were in wireless contact. It was natural that they should. So they thought we knew about Singapore; they thought we were fighting on because we were so brave.'

'Give me your arm, Dave.'

'No, please, sir, *listen*. Unless those Jap officers were positive we had no contact outside, they would never have made up such an outrageous story. And there was no way for them to be positive. Don't you see what I mean? They thought we knew about Singapore.'

Kerr shook his head impatiently. 'It makes no bloody difference one way or the other.'

'It makes all the difference, sir.'

'All right, if you think so. Now give me your arm.'

'Sir, we've got to talk about this.'

'Later.'

'No, it'll be too late.'

'We'll talk about it outside, Dave. Now give me your arm. That's an order! We're wasting time. Let's get outside.'

'Sir—'

'For Christ's sake, Dave, do I have to bloody well arrest you to make you listen? We'll talk outside! Now give me your arm!'

Heavy with despair, Cornish did as he was told.

The first few steps were laboured and agonizing. Kerr's face was a portrait of pain; the corners of his mouth trembled; his eyes were fierce with agony.

As he emerged into the sunlight, however, he found strength to pull himself erect. He saw his men; they saw him. At once the word sped from trench to trench. A cheer, ragged, yet marvellously warm and genuine, burst from the men. Ernie was back; mad old Ernie....

Kerr grinned hugely at them, reviving in the glow of their greeting. He tugged the pipe from his pocket and thrust it between his teeth. Another cheer.

Then the men started to call to him. And Kerr tried to speak to each one. He began to walk, leaning heavily on Cornish's arm. The men cheered anew. Old Ernie was their symbol of invincibility. As long as Mad Old Ernie was alive and kicking, the Japs had failed ...

'You all right now, sir?'

'Of course I am, lad. Never felt better.'
'Glad you got up in time for the show, sir.'
'Had to see what you rascals were up to.'
'Welcome back, sir.'
'Thank you, lad, thank you.'

Cornish felt curiously excluded. It was like being a spectator at a meeting of lovers. Now he knew how the plain friends of attractive girls felt.

'We're ready for 'em, sir.'

A row of faces. Young men's faces. But young men's faces lined and etched, aged too rapidly. A parade of tattered shirts. Bony knees and spindly arms, the fat soaked off them. Sweat streamed down the men's faces as if their steel helmets had been full of sweat when they donned them. And the men smiled at Kerr. They looked happy, the poor devils. Cornish wanted to scream at them: You fools! You're allowing yourselves to be deluded! Don't smile! Please don't smile!

Kerr stationed himself on a hillock beside the road. He sighed as he sank to the ground. His eyes closed for a moment. Cornish thought he had passed out.

'Are you all right, sir?'

Kerr nodded; a moment later he opened his eyes. 'Aye, no need to fret, lad,' he smiled. He put on his glasses and peered down the slope. 'Quiet.'

Cornish watched the second hand of his watch jerk its way around the dial behind the cracked glass. Moments running away, escaping for ever. How many moments left? And after them, what? He remembered the watch in its presentation case, its metal undulled, its fresh leather strap unmarred by a black and filthy sweat-band. Perhaps, a year or two after the war, his father would see a man wearing a watch and tell him, 'I say, that looks remarkably like a watch I had made for my son one Christmas before the war.' And the man would say, 'Really? I took it from the wrist of a dead Jap when we re-occupied Malaya.' End of story.

'Sir,' he said. 'Singapore has fallen. I am convinced the Japs were telling the truth.'

Kerr smiled, still gazing down into the valley. 'I'm not convinced, lad.'

Cornish said, 'But when you start thinking about it—'

'Then don't,' said Kerr. Still smiling.

'But the Japs didn't think for a moment that we didn't know. That's why they were *surprised*—'

'It's a good rule in war,' said Kerr, 'never to start thinking what the enemy wants you to think.' He adjusted his glasses and rested his chin on his folded arms, making himself more comfortable, tacitly stating that he wasn't going to move for a while, not for the enemy, nor for a lot of specious arguments.

'What's the time?'

'Time? Three o'clock, sir.'

With a heavy chuckle, Kerr said, 'I presume you mean fifteen hundred hours, Captain.'

Oh Christ. Cornish turned away. What was the point?

Rifle bolts opened and closed with the sound of bus tickets being punched.

The troops waited.

But the enemy didn't come.

Cornish leant against a tree. His hand broke away a section of the soft bark and tiny ant-like creatures in their hundreds rushed away in alarm.

'I'm sorry,' Cornish said to the insects. 'I didn't mean to disturb you.'

Did you do everything possible to convince Major Kerr that Singapore had fallen?

Yes. I explained, carefully, the reasoning that had led me to that conclusion. But it was futile. He simply didn't want to hear.

Why do you suppose that was?

I don't know ... but I think it was a question of his sense of duty and his undoubtedly courageous nature combining to permit him to see only one course of action.

What about the other officers and the men? Did none of them come to the same conclusions?

Apparently not. They loved him. They cheered themselves hoarse for him even though all he had to offer them was yet another attack by a vastly superior enemy. In a way, Major Kerr had created those men. He had convinced them that they were better than the Japs and the poor sods could hardly wait to prove him right again and again.

Cornish shook his head. Dully, he watched one of the insects running frantically down his arm, over his wrist, along one finger. Gently he flicked it away.

Some of the men had taken off their helmets and stared glumly into the valley, chins resting on their arms; they yawned, apparently losing interest in the proceedings.

Tom Byrne's pith helmet emerged from a trench.

'David, would you mind telling a terrified old cleric just what is going on? I thought we were going to start the shooting again.'

'I think your hat scared the Japs away.'

Tom grinned. 'How's the major?'

'Up and more or less about.'

'How are you?'

'Me?' He frowned, shrugged. 'I'm confused,' he said. 'I've just found out that logic is no match for emotion. But I imagine that's an old story to you.' He glanced down at a man snoring peacefully in the shade of the trench breastwork; he looked as if he hadn't a care in the world. Perhaps he hasn't, Cornish thought. 'The men would follow Kerr anywhere,' he told Tom Byrne. 'If he asked them to march to Tokyo, they'd do it.'

'He's a fine officer.'

'Yes, but our ammo is getting dangerously low; the rifles are worn out, the Brens—oh hell, you don't want to hear about it.'

'What do you want me to say?'

'I don't know.'

'I gather you don't quite agree with the way the major is conducting things.'

'You might say that.'

'But he is your commanding officer, David. And your duty is to him—'

'Yes, that's the order of things, isn't it? The neat arrangement. The system. Mustn't mess around with the bloody system, must we?'

'I know it seems hard at times, but without systems nothing can work.'

Cornish felt savage with frustration. 'You should know, Tom. You have the biggest bloody system of all. A great big set of rules in the sky. Obey them slavishly and you need never trouble your poor little inadequate brain with another doubt as long as you live.'

'David—'

The desire to strike was too strong. 'To start any old religion you just need a chap like Kerr, don't you? A chap with charisma, the ability to get the flock to follow along. Just pop an old cloak on his shoulders and you're all set—'

'Please, David, don't talk like that.'

'Why the hell not?' Cornish glared at the priest. 'It's the truth, isn't it? And isn't the truth what you pretend to be so bloody keen on?'

17

The hours passed. Day became night: a night of waiting, of staring, of wondering. And in the morning the sun rose and nothing had changed except that the Jap bodies on the slope were a little more bloated, a little more evil-smelling.

The British troops looked at one another and shrugged. What the hell was the Jap up to now? Had he given up the hill as a bad job and decided to bypass it? Below, no infantry massed for assault; no artillery barked; no bombers roared overhead. The only sign of life down there was a handful of Japs walking away from the hill, in shirt sleeves. They walked in a relaxed, cheerful manner, like men strolling off to work. Whistling, perhaps, like the Seven Dwarfs.

Kerr returned to his bunk set in the entrance to the cave. He declared that he had had an excellent night's sleep and felt much the better for it.

'But I'm disappointed in the Japs,' he said. 'With all their faults, I did think them to be men of their word. But they let me down. You can't rely on anything these days, can you?'

The troops laughed. Good old Ernie.

Shortly before ten, someone shouted, 'Look!'

All eyes snapped to the slope, hands reaching for rifles as imaginations painted pictures of tidal waves of infantry, bayonets drawn, hurling themselves up the hill.

But there were just six men.

The same men. Two officers; four riflemen, one carrying a white flag.

'He's brought the morning post,' said a Scot as the party drew nearer.

Cornish squinted against the sun. Yes, there was an envelope in Watanabe's hand. He stood up. 'No shooting,' he told Milne who loudly passed the word. He watched Watanabe. What now? Why hadn't the Japs attacked when they said they would?

He went forward to meet the Japanese. Again the solemn unbuckling of sword belts, the bows, the greetings, the bitter smell of sweat and fear and uncertainty.

'Good morning, Captain.'

'Good morning.' The tiniest hint of a smile touched Watanabe's lips. It faded instantly as he asked permission to speak to Cornish's commanding officer.

'Will you wait here, please?'

'Of course. Thank you.' More bows.

Cornish turned to perform his part of the ritual. Brisk steps along the road to the cave. Salute for Kerr. Permission requested; permission granted. Nods. Salutes. About turns.

The Tommies watched it as tourists viewing an incomprehensible but moderately enjoyable ceremony.

Kerr was sitting up in his bunk when the Japanese entered the cave.

Watanabe bowed. 'It is an honour to speak to you again, sir. I am in your debt.'

Kerr nodded. 'You are that,' he said.

'My task is not an easy one,' said Watanabe, opening the envelope. 'I know this must be a matter of great ... importance to you. I feel, however, that I must present these photographs. They were taken, sir, during the signing of the surrender documents and during the occupation of the city of Singapore. I bring these photographs to you in order to prove to you that I told the truth when I said that Singapore had fallen to our forces.'

Kerr ignored the prints; he didn't take them; he didn't even look at them. Watanabe held them for some moments, then put them down on the bunk, delicately, as if fearing they might break.

'I don't believe you,' said Kerr flatly.

'Sir ... the photographs.'

'And I don't believe your bloody photographs either. It's not very hard to fake photographs, Captain.' Kerr's finger stabbed the air. 'You Japs are such an industrious bunch of buggers; I'm sure you'd find it easy.'

'Sir, I can assure you—'

'Aye, I'm sure you can. Well, I can assure you too, my friend. I can assure you that I don't fall for your little trick.'

'It's no trick, sir. Believe me.'

Cornish looked down. The top photographs depicted British soldiers with hands held high, diminutive Japanese guards with rifles and fixed bayonets. They're not fakes, he said to himself. He wanted to say it aloud but he didn't. Surely Kerr would have to accept the truth.

Kerr said, 'I don't blame you for trying it. Just the sort of thing I'd have tried myself if our positions had been reversed. But it didn't work, Captain. Hard luck.'

'But, sir, please study the photograph of General Percival at the conference table with General Yamashita. We could not counterfeit such a photograph.'

Kerr waved an impatient hand.

'Let's not waste any more time with this bullshit, Captain. You tell me a story and I choose not to believe it. We have a difference of opinion.'

Watanabe sighed; his eyes caught Cornish's for an instant. But he had to talk to Kerr; he was the man who had to be convinced. 'Sir, my commanding officer has instructed me to say to you that you have defended this position with a courage and skill eminently worthy of the proud tradition of British arms. There are many of my comrades who have fallen....'

'Aye, I thought I saw a few.'

'Already, sir, you have held this position infinitely longer than anyone might have expected. You have fought magnificently. But, sir, there is no *reason* to fight any more.'

'Is that so?'

'Yes, sir, it is indeed so. Singapore has fallen, sir, thus there is no point in your continuing to fight.' Watanabe wet his lips nervously. 'Please excuse my frankness, sir, when I say that your continued defence is not accomplishing anything. The position has no value any more. It is simply a ... a pocket of resistance which must be ... eliminated eventually. It is not our intention to do anything with this position when we take it—'

'*If* you take it, you mean.'

Watanabe seemed to be cursing himself for not being able to convey this obvious truth. 'Sir, it makes no sense for men to die for a position that has no value.'

'I agree,' said Kerr. 'So bloody well stop fighting.'

Watanabe's hands were open as if in an attempt to communicate. 'Sir, may I point out just how utterly hopeless your position is.'

'Aye,' said Kerr. 'I'd like to hear.'

'Thank you. You are of course completely surrounded. You have no hope of supply or reinforcement because there is no one left to supply or reinforce you. Your ammunition cannot last forever, sir, no matter how much you brought in your lorries and on your mules. My commanding officer told me—and, sir, I quote him precisely—"It is time for good sense to prevail. While Singapore held out there was a reason for you to continue the fight. We understood your motives. We respected them. Now there is no reason to fight on. It is time to think of men's lives."'

'Jap lives.'

'And English lives, sir. You have lost many men already. It is wrong that men should die for no reason.'

'I agree.'

Watanabe looked uncertainly at Kerr. 'If we agree, sir, then surely we might decide on a course of action.'

'A good idea.' Kerr sucked at his empty pipe, clearly enjoying himself. 'First, I will tell you my course of action and then you can tell me your course of action. Now my course of action is quite simple. I am going to kill all the bloody Japs who come up here and try and take *my* position. Now, what is your course of action?'

Watanabe's face fell. He nodded slowly as if telling himself that there was nothing more he could accomplish. He said, 'Sir, we will hold our fire until twelve noon in order that you may give the matter more thought. If by that time we have heard nothing from you, we shall resume hostilities and more men will die for no purpose.'

'My compliments to your commanding officer,' said Kerr cheerfully. 'We'll hold our fire until noon too.'

Watanabe bowed. 'Thank you, sir, I shall convey your remarks and your compliments.'

Men are never so courteous, Cornish thought, as when they are preparing to slaughter one another.

They stood on the road near the blackened carcass of the tank. Before them the squad of Japanese soldiers waited with flat, impassive faces. Their eyes avoided the eyes of the British troops who studied them with genial contempt.

'What I said was true,' said Watanabe.

Cornish nodded and stared glumly at the boots of the Japanese riflemen.

'Your Major Kerr is a brave man. You are all brave men.

But this continued resistance is ... ill advised. It serves no purpose.'

'The decision is his,' said Cornish.

'I understand. But you will learn that I have told you the truth. Singapore has fallen, Captain, I can assure you.'

'Major Kerr finds that very difficult to believe.'

'And you do not?'

'I didn't say that.'

'No, of course. Forgive my presumption. I too found it very difficult to believe the news when first I heard it. I told my radio man to obtain confirmation. I thought, frankly, that it might be some clever trick of yours.'

No, Cornish thought flatly, we have no tricks. He said, 'You will understand that I cannot comment on my commanding officer's statement.'

'I understand.'

'We will examine the photographs.'

'Please do. They are genuine. As a matter of fact,' said Watanabe, with a tiny perplexed smile, 'it was a surprise to learn that you did not know of Singapore's fall. We assumed you would be in radio contact.'

'One of your shells was particularly well placed.'

'I see.' Watanabe turned and looked at the soldiers standing nearby. 'These are the bravest men we have encountered in Malaya. You have every right to feel proud of them.'

Cornish nodded a curt acknowledgement.

Salutes, bows, dust kicked up by stamping heels: the Japanese were gone.

When Cornish returned to the cave he discovered that the photographs had been destroyed.

'Why?'

'They were rubbish.'

'I wanted to examine them.'

'It would have been a waste of time.'

'How do you know?'

Kerr smiled, the patient teacher. 'I told you: never do what the enemy wants you to do, never think what he wants you to think. Always think and do something else. Keep him off balance, keep him guessing. I forget who told me that but it was good advice; I've always remembered it. The Japs *want* us to worry about Singapore, so we won't.'

Cornish said coldly, 'We can't ignore the truth for ever.'

Kerr's face darkened. 'You don't know it's the truth.'

'I'm sure it is.'

'Well, I'm bloody well sure it isn't. Is that clear?'

'Perfectly clear, sir.'

Kerr cleared his throat and scratched his nose. 'You'll find I'm right, you know.'

'I hope so.'

Unexpectedly, Kerr chuckled. 'You let that Jap bastard rattle you, Dave. It's easily done, but we mustn't let ourselves be taken in by the sods. We know they'd dearly love us to throw up our hands and surrender; it'd save them no end of trouble. So what's more natural than for them to try and concoct some story to try and make us give up? I don't blame them; I'd do the same if I was in their boots.'

Cornish said, 'Sir, I know you don't want to believe it but—'

'We have to be here,' said Kerr as if Cornish hadn't spoken, 'when they start the push back north. And they will. Oh, yes, there's no doubt about it. The question is, when. We're doing an important job here, Dave lad, at a critical time. So for God's sake, don't start letting me down —not now.'

'It's not a question of letting you down.' Cornish sighed. If all else fails, appeal to a public schoolboy's sense of fair play. 'I'm simply stating what seems to me a reasonable opinion.'

'Aye,' Kerr nodded vigorously, 'and I'm glad to have your opinion. Christ, that's why I wanted you for my Number Two in the first place. You have opinions. I've no use for people without 'em. They slide through life without really touching the sides.' His great hands, muscular yet not without grace, curved in the air before him as he spoke. Cornish thought of the hypnotist's watch pendulous on a gold chain ... Was there an element of hypnotism in leadership? Watch the hands at all times.

'I've been a soldier a long time,' said Kerr. 'A hell of a long time. You can't help learning a few things—no matter how hard you try. One thing I've learnt is that things happen to soldiers who *deserve* things to happen. The lads got out at Dunkirk because they deserved to get out. We got reinforced once in 1917 because we deserved it; they got through just in time. Oh, you can pooh-hooh that sort of thing, I know. But I believe it. And we're going to get out of this because we bloody well deserve to!'

'I hope you're right,' said Cornish dully. It was pointless. Kerr would go on to the bloody end, believing precisely what he wanted to believe. Talking with him wasn't dialogue, it was two monologues passing each other, like two birds going in opposite directions.

18

The men paraded.

Lines of scarecrows, their uniforms rotting on their thin bodies, their skin burnt and leathery, many with feet wrapped in blanket strips, many more with sores and blisters.

But they held their chins high.

Sergeant Firmin walked along the ranks. 'You're a sorry-looking bloody shower,' he said, touching a tattered sleeve here, a ragged pocket there.

'Confidentially, Sarn't,' said a private with a bandaged left arm, 'you don't look too bleedin' gorgeous yourself.'

Dressing was painful but Kerr was determined to look his best.

'Is my tunic all right at the back? Does it show, the spot where the bloody mortar went through? Pull the tunic down, will you, so that it covers the mend.'

Cornish did as he was asked.

Kerr handed him a slip of paper. 'Now, give me a test, Dave. Let me think. Private Hibley, V.T., and Private Rowbotham, M.W. Hibley is from London, Ealing, I think. A baker before the war. Married. Two children. His wife's name is ... don't tell me ... Mary.'

'Martha,' said Cornish, looking at the notes.

'Bugger. Yes, Martha. Martha, Martha, Martha. I won't forget it again. The other lad is Rowbotham. From Nottingham. Not married. Nineteen. His dad works in the railway. Am I right?'

'Yes, quite right.'

Kerr chuckled. 'Bloody nuisance, learning all that stuff. But worth it. Go up to a man and start talking about his missus, Martha or Mary or whatever the hell her name is, and you've made a friend for life. Oh Christ, he knows perfectly well you looked it up just a few minutes ago. But you *did* look it up. That's the point. You took the trouble, because of him; see what I mean? A man gets a nice warm feeling when an officer talks to him as an individual instead of just another bod in khaki, a number; that's what he gets all the time, in the army. You talk to him as a man and he'll serve you ten times better because of it. And that's what matters, isn't it?'

'I suppose so,' said Cornish.

'Suppose so? No suppose about it. An officer's function is to make the most efficient force of the men under his command. He leads them. And leading is a bloody sight more than just standing up and waving your sword and yelling, "Charge!"'

'I'm sure they'd charge if you asked them.'

Kerr glanced down at Cornish.

'D'you think these men are exceptional?'

'Of course.'

'Of course, nothing. Men are men; soldiers are soldiers and they're all alike. They average out. You get some dim ones and some bright ones and you usually get 'em in about the same quantities. I imagine all armies do. The French, the Germans, the Russians, the Yanks. Even the Japs. They all average out because they're full of average men. It's the officers who make the difference. It's the officers who make them what they are: good, bad or bloody awful. And for an officer to make something of men he has to reach them and a hell of a good way is to find out and remember that Private Hibley, V. T., is married to a lass named Martha!'

Cornish half smiled in spite of himself. 'And you told me you were a simple man.'

'That's right, lad, but not simple-minded. Before this lot is over, I might have to learn the name of every man's wife and mother and mistress and grandmother. And it may be worth the effort! That's something they don't teach you at Sandhurst, but it's true! Now, come on, lad, give me your arm. We're going outside.'

Privates Hibley and Rowbotham stood before their comrades, their thin bodies erect, their eyes set firmly on the distant hills.

'I'm very proud of you two,' Kerr boomed, 'and I'm grateful to the Japs for giving me an opportunity to say so in front of you all.' He stood with his back against the shattered stump of a giant tree, his left hand gripping the surface and taking some of the weight of his body. The pain was evident in his eyes but his mouth kept curving into obstinate smiles 'These men performed acts of great bravery,' he declared, 'which will be rewarded at the proper time in the appropriate manner. Hibley here rescued a comrade in the face of fierce enemy fire. And Rowbotham personally attacked a party of Japs who managed to reach our positions. Brave men. And I'm deeply proud of them.' He turned to look at the two privates but his voice didn't diminish in volume. 'Martha's going to be as pleased as punch to hear about this, isn't she? Are you thinking of going back to being a baker when this is all over?'

'I ... dunno, sir,' gulped Hibley, flushing with pleasure.

'Never mind, lad. Plenty of time to make your mind up about that.' He turned to the nineteen-year-old. 'Your dad will be telling all his mates at the railway about you. And so he should! All Nottingham will soon hear what you've done here!' He placed his hands on his hips. 'Break ranks,' he told the entire assembly. 'Gather round. Let's have a chat about things.'

The chat was a success. Kerr told the men about the visit of the Japanese. He told them that he was a little disappointed because when he had seen the white flag approaching he had naturally assumed that the Japs were at last coming to their senses and were surrendering. The men roared. Kerr flattered them outrageously. He told them how the Japs had sent their best troops to try and dislodge them from the hill, how they had been reduced to shabby little tricks in an attempt to do the job.

'It's not bull,' declared Kerr, 'when I tell you that you're all members of the world's most exclusive club: the defenders of this stinking, rotten, glorious hill! Your names will go down in history. Oh yes, believe me, they will. Kiddies will thrill to the sound of your names because they'll be on a par with Lawrence and Shackleton and Bishop and Ball. I'm just grateful, bloody sincerely grateful, that I've been given the privilege of serving with you!'

Even the cynics found themselves responding. There was something so overwhelmingly natural about the way Kerr spoke. It was like listening to 'Land of Hope and Glory'. Your heart surged even as your intellect wrote it off as a lot of bull.

'And what of the future? Are we going to stay here the rest of the war?' Kerr asked his men. 'Dear me no, we are not. Soon we will be reinforced and supplied. By air or ground; I don't know which; all I know is, help will come. And then it won't be too bloody long until *we'll* be the ones doing the attacking! And when that time comes, we'll push the little bastards back into the sea and put paid to them once and for all! Christ, he attacked us without warning. We weren't ready for him. We had to fall back ... a hell of a long way, as you know. But we're not falling back any more, lads. That's all over and done with. The Jap's had his bit of success. Now he's going to pay the price for it!'

Cornish clasped his fingers behind him. He felt the sweat running over them, from finger to finger, like warm glue that would soon cool and set. He wished Major Kerr would die now, with these men present....

'Yes, we're surrounded!' Kerr bellowed. 'We're encircled. Just like an oak tree is encircled—by grass and by weeds and by little crawling ants that try like hell to get up the tree but can't!'

The men cheered. Kerr's eyes filled with tears that spilled down his cheeks. His lips trembled. He saluted the men; he nodded as he saluted. The men swarmed about him, their thin faces and bright eyes on him. They wanted to be near to greatness.

'You're bloody mad,' said Gibbs.

'Just patch me up.' Kerr's voice was weak and husky. 'Bugger the commentaries.'

'I told you to lie down and stay down.'

'I know. And I didn't. I'm a naughty boy. Now, for Christ's sake, shut up about it. Patch me up. Stop bleating like a bloody old woman.'

'I'm trying to keep you alive.'

'I know, I know.'

'And you're doing your level best to bloody well kill yourself!'

'I'll be good, I promise.'

Gibbs worked on the wound for fifteen minutes. When he had finished he told Kerr that if he moved he would probably bleed to death. 'See that he lies still,' he told McGregor.

'Aye, sir,' said McGregor, reddening.

Cornish followed Gibbs outside.

'Is it true that he might bleed to death?'

'Lord, yes. I'm surprised he hasn't already. I suppose he's too bloody obstinate. He's extraordinarily brave, you know. I really don't know how he managed to stand up and talk to the men. He must have been in agony.'

'He has divine powers.'

'What?'

'Nothing. Is he fit to continue in command?'

'Christ, no, of course not.'

'But he won't relinquish command.'

'I can't make him. Why, do you think he should relinquish command?'

'Yes, I think he's becoming irrational.'

'I suppose we all are in one way or another.'

'He's talking about reinforcements and supplies...'

'Well?'

'He knows damn well we'll never be reinforced or supplied.'

'What do you mean?'

'There's no one left to reinforce us or supply us.'

'What?'

'Singapore has fallen, Mike.'

'No.'

'Yes, it has.'

'*Singapore?* You can't be serious.'

'It's difficult to believe, isn't it?'

'Impossible.'

'Keep trying. It gets easier the longer you keep at it.'

And no one influenced you in your decision?

No one.

No one even suggested it to you?

No. It was entirely my decision.

Doesn't it strike you as singular that of all the men on

the hill, only you thought to precipitate such an action?

No. I was in a better position than most of the men to realize what was happening.

And what was happening? Do you know? Have you managed to work it all out?

I think so. I have thought about it very carefully and I have come to the conclusion that a gallant officer was squandering his courage and the lives of his men to no purpose. He refused, however, to accept that fact. Why? Because he wanted—no, he needed—to believe that there was significance in this action, that it mattered. It was incredibly important to him, you see. After all, this was it: at last: the opportunity to prove himself. And he had waited so long.

19

Cornish laid the bullets before him. Six of them, each .38-inch calibre, in a dully metallic row. He took the first bullet, rolled it slowly between his fingers, then slid it into an empty chamber in the revolver. It fitted snugly, perfectly. As he reached for the second bullet, he observed the steadiness of his hand. How very Boy's-Own-paper, he thought, remembering an illustration depicting a minute group of Anglo-Saxon heroes calmly loading the last few rounds into their rifles as about three-quarters of a million Zulus bounded down on them with drawn spears.

'Honestly, I'm damned sorry,' he said.

But Kerr wasn't there to hear.

The bullets nestled in the revolver's cylinder, their shiny heads forming a neat pattern of circles.

Insanity.

He shook his head, weary and dejected and afraid. Whatever happened now, he would have lost.

Insanity.

At Liverpool, a man had stood at the gangplank leading up to the troopship. His job was to hand out instruction leaflets advising officers that each was permitted to take up to ten cwt of baggage which should include mess kit. According to the document, officers were at liberty to bring their own horses although it was considered likely that good mounts would be available on most overseas stations. Private cars were transportable but necessitated a great deal of paperwork, similarly special licenses were required for private firearms.

He remembered reading that absurd relic of pre-war. Laughing like hell at the authority that had forgotten to stop handing them out. Still, warming to the sense of adventure, the daring of setting off for foreign shores....

And this was how it would end. In a sort of shame.

Oh hell! He thrust the pistol into its holster. Then he stood up. He looked back. Mike Gibbs's dressing-station clung to the hillside like a disreputable growth. Beyond lay a few dozen more miles of jungle ... and then there was Singapore. Once it had symbolized security and strength; now it was just another place of defeat. He wondered why the Japs didn't simply sit back and wait for the British to starve to death. But perhaps there was professional pride involved. Perhaps the Japanese colonel had promised his general that he would take the place, by force of arms. If so, the promise would of course be worth far more than the lives it would cost to fulfil.

He avoided the path, preferring to make his way across the thick, coarse grass. It was slippery. He fell more than once, the revolver swinging sullenly against his thigh as if prodding him on to do what he called his duty. Christ, how unfair it all was. Why him? Why not someone else? He had no answers to his questions.

Kerr had slept for a few minutes, then a tiny movement had sent a shaft of pain stabbing through him. He awoke, his lips curled back, his teeth trying to bite the pain in half. Then he said 'Sod you' to the pain and relaxed his features. He wouldn't give the pain the satisfaction of a writhing, wriggling reaction. 'Go to hell. Bugger off.' One by one he loosened his fingers' grip on the shaky bamboo chair-arms. He composed himself, lying quite still, breathing only a little more heavily than usual. The sweat ran in deliberate little rivulets down his cheeks, past his mouth, around his chin.

My arse is aflame, he thought, conjuring up pictures of smoke and shooting fire. He wondered if the wound had rendered him impotent. It was possible; any wound in that region could have nasty effects....

Oh well.

He sniffed. He'd done his share—more than his share—in his time.

God, I'd like to *see* a woman, he thought. I don't want to *do* anything to her; hell, I *couldn't*. But I'd love to see a real woman. With big heavy breasts and good lips. I'd love to hear her talk and smell her perfume and...

He thought of the woman in the pub near Hertford. He had stopped at the place on his way to Hull in the Morris. He had a pint of beer and a pork pie. She served him: a bright, smiling creature with hair the colour of bronze. She was the publican's wife and some twenty years his junior. Kerr exchanged a few words with her; for some inexplicable reason they got on to Charlie Chaplin and George Arliss. Mutual favourites of the two of them. The conversation was a delight: one of those wondrous occasions when the dialogue might have been prepared by a master dramatist because every word is perfect and leads to a perfect response. What made the whole thing that much more enjoyable—in a vaguely masochistic way—was the presence of the publican. A plump but rather gloomy-looking man, he stood at one end of the bar while his wife and Kerr chatted and chuckled at the other. Afterwards, Kerr told himself that he and the woman fell in love over the counter with the husband looking on. Kerr stayed until closing time. Quietly, as she wiped the counter in front of him, she told him to drive half a mile down the road and wait. Park this side of the stone bridge, were the instructions. Kerr did so. He waited thirty-five minutes and then she came to him, her hair loose on her shoulders, her face warm with desire. 'We haven't much time, love,' she said, 'so let's not waste any of it. You want me and I want you. Badly. Drive in the lane there behind the trees. No one will see us. I wish you had a bigger car but where there's a will, I always say. Can you unbutton me down the back while you're driving?'

Kerr never returned to the pub near Hertford. The reason was simple: he was afraid of losing a memory that had become inexpressibly dear to him. The talk, the in-step kindling of two strangers' emotions, the splendidly shameless love-making. Better to remember them than try to recreate them; better to have a triumph to recall than a disappointment.

Kerr was faithful to Louise for four years after Brian's death. She didn't believe him but it was true. For four years he nurtured a faint hope that the old life might be rebuilt. Finally, however, the hope evaporated, like the brandy she slopped on the floor. And there was Georgina who had three children, all by different fathers. There was Hilda who favoured frolicking in bubble baths. There was Mrs Lefler who gave him a Dunhill pipe for Christmas and who owned a dress shop in Harrogate and who would turn off the lights and pull down the blinds and display the 'Closed' sign in the middle of the day. There was the city engineer's wife who always said No repeatedly before saying Perhaps, well, just this time. There was the lieutenant-colonel's wife whose problem was that the lieutenant-colonel preferred young men. There was the divorcee with the most delectable breasts who adored being touched everywhere but on her delectable breasts. There was the sweet-faced bitch who borrowed ten pounds and never repaid them.

There was the appealingly ugly girl who was quite sensational in bed. There was the middle-aged lady from Dundee who was even better. There was the girl from Llandudno who was so nervous that she wet the bed. There was the librarian who bit him in odd places. There was the major's wife who reported that he was better endowed than Captain Willoughby-Frazer but not quite as well as Lieutenant Lyttleton. There was Mrs Cooper-Yeadon whose husband commanded a destroyer or a frigate or something. There was Hester.

Christ, he thought as Cornish entered, he looks shaky.

Tension was grabbing Cornish's innards and threatening to pull them apart. He had a very real fear of being sick before he had time to utter a word. The enormity of what he was about to do was like a weight crushing him, stifling him....

Kerr smiled painfully and asked the time.

'My bloody watch has stopped again,' he said. 'Got some dirt in it. I can't imagine how.' He laughed and winced.

'There's an hour to go,' said Cornish carefully.

'Ah.' Kerr wiped his eyes with the tips of his fingers. He did it in a curiously delicate manner as if afraid that his vision might be permanently damaged if it was not done with finesse. 'Thank the Lord we've still got a good bit of ammo. Remember what a bind it was bringing it all, on the mules ... but worth it now, eh?'

Cornish said, 'Are you just going to let the time run out?'

Kerr looked at him with his steady eyes. 'I don't see that we have a hell of a lot of choice, do you?'

Outside, a man laughed, a carefree-sounding laugh, a half-pint-in-the-pub-on-Sunday laugh.

Cornish swallowed. He said, 'I think we have come to the point where we must ask ourselves whether we haven't done everything we can here, whether there's really anything left to gain.'

Kerr ran his tongue over his lips as he appeared to consider the point. 'Aye, well, in the end I suppose it comes down to being a matter of opinion.' He smiled, a friendly-argument-between-equals smile. 'Yours and mine.'

'Men's lives are involved here.'

'Yes. Soldiers' lives. We have a job to do here, Dave.'

'I know but—'

'Sit down, make yourself comfortable.'

'No. I'd rather stand,' Cornish said. 'I'm here to disagree and I disagree better standing up.'

Christ, it sounded so damned schoolboyish ... so tight-lipped, so bringing things to a head, so clearing the air, so knowing where everyone stood. Words he'd once used in arguments about the rugger team were revolving in his brain, the same words, and now they were to be used for a matter of men's lives....

He went on, 'Sir, I honestly believe the only course open to us is to tell the men that those who want to make a run for it may do so and those who want to ... surrender may do so. We should give them the choice. If we don't everyone will die. I think it's as simple and straightforward as that.'

Kerr nodded slowly, sadly. The moments seemed to be weighed down by the sodden air; they dragged by sluggishly, unwillingly. Kerr rubbed his eyes; he looked tired and, suddenly, rather old.

He said, 'They tell me the Japs don't think very bloody much of soldiers who surrender.'

'I know,' said Cornish, 'that's why we have to give the men the opportunity, the choice, of making a run for it.'

'How far will any of them get?'

'God knows but—'

'They won't get very far, Dave.' Kerr spread his hands. He was sweet reasonableness. 'That's only my opinion, of course. I could be wrong. I'm not infallible. I've never pretended to be. But I do have a hell of a lot of experience of soldiering. Now I don't have any experience in advertising, so I don't claim to know anything about it. But soldiering, yes. An old sweat like me gets to be able to smell a situation. And, Christ almighty, I'd be the last man to claim that this isn't a thoroughly dicey situation. It is. Dicey as bloody hell, but—'

'We have ammunition for about one more day!' Cornish felt the anger boiling within him. 'One day, for God's sake!'

'We can make it last.'

'No! Don't you see! We've got to give it to the men who choose to make a run for it.'

Kerr scowled as if he had tasted something foul. 'Run for it? Like frightened little bloody rabbits?'

'If they don't run, everyone will die. For nothing.'

Kerr shook his head slowly at Cornish. 'I suppose you think I'm just a stubborn old bugger. Well, I suppose I am. But, Dave lad, a lot of good men have died for this place. We can't just throw it all away.'

'Is it better to throw away more lives?'

'Besides, there's a rightness in these things. I've seen it more than once. We were trapped once, I remember, outside Loos. Cut off. The Hun was giving us a hell of a rough time. Artillery, machine-guns, anything he could find. And we weren't on top of a hill, but down low. We stuck it out. Our ammo was down to practically nothing. It looked as if it would be hands-up. But the captain, a lad from Birmingham, if I remember right, said he'd become much too fond of the place to give it up. No, by God, he'd fight the Hun with his bare fists if necessary! Well, we hung on a bit longer. And it was just long enough. They got through to us just as we were sticking our last clips in. We were saved!'

'And everyone lived happily ever after.'

'What?'

'Nothing.' Cornish shook his head. It was no time to discuss the moral implications of military folklore. 'We only have a little time left.'

'They'll get through to us, Dave lad, I know they will.'

'Who will?'

'The main force, from the south.'

Cornish stared. 'Christ, there *isn't* a main force any more!'

'Of course there is—'

'No!'

'Dave, you mustn't let yourself believe that crap about Singapore being lost .... and those fake snapshots.'

'They weren't fakes.'

'Oh, yes, they were, Dave, believe me.'

'No, sir, I'm sorry, I don't believe you.'

'You prefer to believe the Japs, do you?'

Cornish's head pounded. 'Sir, you're a brave, brave man ... but you're not being realistic, for God's sake. You're thinking in terms of the relief of Mafeking or something. Don't you see, this bloody country is full of Japs; God, we're probably the only British troops left fighting. The only way to get to us is by air ... and there hasn't been the slightest indication that the R.A.F. is still in existence. We haven't seen a British plane for weeks. How can you possibly think they're going to reinforce us?'

Kerr sighed. 'It's our duty to fight on,' he said.

'Until the last man?'

'If necessary, yes.'

'Simple, isn't it?'

'Yes, simple,' said Kerr, looking down at his hands.

'That's the way you like things, don't you, sir?'

Kerr didn't answer for a moment. Then he said 'Yes,' in a soft tone. He continued to look at his hands for a few moments, then he glanced up. 'You'd best get back to your men,' he said.

Cornish almost turned and went. The dismissal had been so matter-of-fact, so normal, so everyday. So bloody kindly. It was a reminder that everything was still afloat, that he hadn't rocked things too violently, not yet.

'Are you waiting for something?'

Cornish wavered. It was the moment of truth. Now or never. Act now, for there will never be another chance. Am I right? he asked himself. Yes. I am right, I am, he told himself, as if already defending his action.

His right hand dropped toward the holster. It took an eternity: an eternity in which he saw Kerr's eyes following the movement of his hand: an eternity in which he considered abandoning the whole thing and simply sticking the offending hand in his pocket.

Then his fingers touched the revolver's pebbly grip. A voice, shrill with horrified incredulity, demanded to know whether he fully realized what he was doing.

His fingers curled around the grip. His thumb nudged the hammer. The gun came free. It felt huge in his hand. He gripped it tightly, fearful of it slipping from his sweaty fingers.

'Sir,' he said, his voice strained and awkward, 'I consider that your actions have become irrational in regard to the defence of this position. I am therefore relieving you of command. I deeply regret this but it is necessary to avoid further bloodshed.'

Kerr gazed at him. 'Don't be a bloody fool, Dave.'

He spoke in the friendly, casual manner of a man advising a chum not to bet five shillings on a particular horse.

'I'm sorry,' Cornish said again. 'I'm doing this only because I know it is absolutely necessary.'

'No, no,' Kerr said. 'Don't do it. Christ, you'll regret it for the rest of your life.'

'It's necessary, sir.'

Kerr frowned and looked away. Then, with a sigh, he said, 'Well, have you thought it all out, telling the men what you've done, telling them that you've stuck me up with a gun like a bloody gangster? Have you thought about that? And what are your orders now, Mr Cornish? I'd like to know, now that I'm under your command.'

Cornish said, 'Please don't be flippant about this, sir. Believe me, I have enormous respect for you ...'

'That was what the Jap said. Interesting, the two of you both saying the same thing.' Kerr smiled.

'If you want to consider me a traitor, that's your affair. But I'm not. I only want to save lives.'

'He said that too.'

Cornish felt the sweat running into his eyes. 'Sir, I'm going to address the men. Explain the situation. Give them the option of making a dash for it or staying.'

'And you?'

'I'm going to stay. Someone has to stay with the wounded.'

'And you're going to give the hill to the Japs.'

'We have no choice.'

'We do. We can fight like soldiers. That's what we're here to do, in case you'd forgotten.'

'I hadn't forgotten.'

Kerr half grinned. 'Christ, Dave, look, I know how it is. I've felt the courage leaking out of me....'

'It's not a question of courage. Honestly. I've thought about it endlessly. It took more courage to pull this pistol on you than face the Jap army. You probably don't believe that but it's true. And I do respect you—much more than perhaps you can understand. But the point is, we've fought for this bloody hill so long it's become a reason in itself.'

'The men still have fighting spirit.'

'I know. They're magnificent. Magnificent because you've convinced them that they're magnificent. They'll do anything you ask of them because they think you're the next thing to Winston Churchill. They love you. But they'll all die—'

'We'll get help.'

'No, we won't! We won't! We can't! For Christ's sake, understand that! You're deluding yourself just as you're deluding the men. Don't you see ...'

Kerr turned away as if the sight of Cornish pained him. 'I didn't expect this of you.'

'I know you didn't. And I'm sorry. But this damned hill isn't worth another life.'

'Has it ever occurred to you that it might be much more than just this hill?'

'What do you mean?'

'I mean, we're holding up a sizeable portion of the Jap army, stopping it dead in its tracks—'

'No, that doesn't matter any more!'

'Don't you see, Dave, if we stop the bastards, then we may give another unit a chance to catch its breath and that may give another lot an opportunity to organize something else. Christ, any victory is made up of the work of God-knows-how-many units, all fighting and winning ... Why, what we do here, Dave, might be the *turning point* ... don't you see that?'

'You're deceiving yourself. You're believing what you want to believe. Singapore has fallen!'

'No. I will not believe that.'

'It's true, sir,' Cornish said. 'Please believe me ...'

'Call yourself a soldier.'

'No, I don't. I'm not a soldier. I don't want to be one.'

'You're a mummy's boy, *Captain* Cornish. You're wearing a soldier's suit but you're a bloody imposter! No stomach, *Captain* Cornish, that's your trouble! You should never have left your precious advertising business. Baby soap and bog paper: that's your style, *Captain* Cornish! You should have stuck to them!'

Kerr's scorn seemed to burn into Cornish's eyes. 'I don't want to have to bind you,' he said carefully. 'I'm therefore going to ask you to stay here while I address the troops.'

'And what are you going to say to them, *Captain* Cornish?'

'I've told you that already.'

'They'll ask about me, you know.'

'I shall say that you have relinquished command due to wounds.'

Kerr spat.

Cornish tried to move aside in time but the spittle caught him on the cheek. He felt it sliding down like some vile slug.

Kerr moved. Slowly, painfully. He put his feet on the floor. His eyes closed briefly, then opened again. Deep breath.

'Don't move,' said Cornish.

Kerr didn't answer. He looked past Cornish as he pushed his agonized body upright.

Cornish felt sick. His flesh burned. Sweat created a slimy film between his hand and the revolver.

Now Kerr stood before him, rocking slightly, his breath loud and laboured. He started to move towards Cornish.

'Stay there! I'll shoot!'

'No, you won't.'

'I will ... I swear ...'

'Give me the gun, lad.'

'No, I ...'

But already Kerr's hand was grasping the barrel. Pull the trigger, Cornish told himself. Pull the bloody thing! Now!

It was too late. Gently but firmly, Kerr twisted the gun from Cornish's hand.

'That's better.'

Cornish gulped. And, then, violently, he flung himself to the side of the cave and vomited. Through his heavings he heard Kerr commenting on the sight. Unpleasant: shame the lad couldn't keep down his breakfast: a soldier should have a strong stomach.

At last it was over. Weakly, Cornish turned and wiped his mouth. Kerr stood over him, vast with anger. He held the revolver in his right hand.

'I'm going to shoot you,' he said.

Cornish nodded, absorbing the intelligence in numbed silence. He looked at the muzzle of the pistol. It was cold and grey and rock steady.

'I told you not to,' said Kerr, as if discussing the outcome of the five-shilling bet.

Immediately to the right of the barrel was the snubby metallic nose of the bullet that would tear its way through him. He had held it in his hand; he had thrust it into the chamber. Now it was going to kill him.

'Where would you like it?'

Cornish looked up. 'What?'

'I said, Mr Bloody-Advertising-Man-Dressed-Up-As-A-Soldier, where would you like the bullet?'

'Where ...?'

'Nice of me, eh? You weren't going to give me any choice. Just a round in the gut for me. But I'm giving you the chance to state your preference. Under the circumstances I think it's rather a gentlemanly thing for me to do, don't you?'

The revolver was only an inch from Cornish's eyes.

'Well?'

The words built up within him like water straining at a dam wall. Words of pleading. Begging for mercy. But no ... hell, no, he wouldn't let them out. He wouldn't give the bastard the pleasure of hearing them ... He would hang on to the one last vestige of dignity ...

Numbly he wondered why it mattered to him, at this last moment.

'Between the eyes? Very quick that way. You'll hardly feel it. A bang and it'll be all over. Or in the heart? Would you prefer that? Not so messy. Haven't you got anything to say about it?'

Cornish shook his head, not trusting himself to speech.

The barrel of the pistol came closer. It was gigantic in his eyes. He turned his head but still he felt its presence. It seemed to burn the air. In a moment, he told himself, it will all be over. Hang on, please hang on ... don't break now....

'All right, you're going to leave it up to me, are you?'

I beg you to hurry and I beg you to wait....

'I'm within my rights, you know. You threatened me with a firearm. Sorry, Dave.'

Oh Christ, it's now. Kerr's breathing: great heavings of air: the last thing he would hear on earth. Hold on....

'Here goes.'

Cornish nodded dumbly, his eyes tightly closed, his flesh contracting in anticipation of the awful blow.

The gun cracked like thunder in the confined space.

Pain ... streaking ... burning ... noise, deafening, shattering ...

Eyes open. The cave wall still there. Dull rumbling pain in the thigh.

And Kerr was there. Smiling, the bastard. Revolver in hand. Barrel smoking.

Cornish stared. Suddenly the pain ceased. He seemed to be unconnected with the untidy looking specimen on the floor of the cave, pouring blood through his rotten, sun-bleached khaki.

Footsteps. It was McGregor, his peasant face wide with alarm.

'You all right, sir?'

'Yes, but poor Captain Cornish has hurt himself.'

Poor Captain Cornish.

'His gun went off accidentally.'

'I'll get the M.O., sir.'

'Yes. Hurry. The poor feller is in some pain.'

'Aye, sir.'

The voices sounded distant. They seemed to echo and have tiny reverberations, as if they were being transmitted by some metal device.

'And ask Captain Milne to come here.'

'Aye, sir.'

More footsteps. Everyone seemed to be in a hell of a hurry.

Kerr: 'Strangest thing: you hit yourself in just the same spot I was hit.' He was grinning down at Cornish but his eyes were steady. 'A bit of bad luck, that.'

Cornish nodded.

'But it could have been a bloody sight worse, couldn't it?'

Cornish nodded again. Yes, Major Kerr, I agree, Major Kerr. See, I am still nodding, Major Kerr, anything you say, Major Kerr....

'You might even say that you were a bloody sight luckier than you deserved to be.'

Yes, yes, yes. Lucky as hell. You are absolutely right,

Major Kerr. As always. God, but I feel tired, he thought. Perhaps I am dying, even though Kerr shot me in the thigh instead of in the head or the heart. Shame, to die from a thigh wound. But it doesn't make that much difference, one way or the other. I'm going to die anyway. The Japs. Oddly enough, I had forgotten all about them for some minutes. But it doesn't matter now. It will all be over in the not-too-distant future: End of the Incredibly Important Existence of David Edward Cornish. Poor Pater: no son left to carry on the glorious family enterprise; poor Mater: she will manage somehow to blame it on the Jews.

'You're making an awful bloody mess on my floor. But I wouldn't touch the wound if I were you. Wait till the M.O. comes. He won't be long.' Kerr sounded almost chatty.

And then Kerr was talking to other men and the voices became vague and disjointed. Cornish felt himself nodding and continuing to nod. It seemed terribly important to keep expressing total agreement with the commuter of the death sentence ... a gift of a bit more life, albeit with a chunk of lead in the rear end ... in a world that consists of a long grey tube down which one must travel, spinning slowly like a leaf in a lazy stream and saying Good Morning to a series of people who look vaguely like relatives and friends and shop clerks and copywriters and art directors and photographers and clients and prospective clients and former clients and clients' wives and Grade A girls enlisted to make clients' visits to London that much pleasanter and that much more memorable: smooth metallic faces with alert painted smiles beneath vacant eyes ... and hands reaching out to catch one but one has to keep spinning on one's way down the long grey tube and the faces are left far behind and in front is a giant turd that is pretending to be a snubby-nosed bullet sliding into the barrel....

20

Kerr was saddened. It was grim, seeing a man come to pieces like a jig-saw puzzle. It was worse, far worse, than seeing him killed, because all the respect you had for him turned sour inside you instead of becoming sweet sadness. Cornish had disintegrated; there was no other way to describe it. Kerr thought how close he had come to killing him—he had deserved it, the traitorous bastard. God knows how he had managed to end up with a bullet in the arse instead of in the head.

Kerr sighed. Milne had taken over as Number Two. He had been properly grateful and eager when told the news. Milne wouldn't disintegrate; you could be sure of that. He was too bloody dense.

Kerr stared bleakly at the grubby *atap* against the wall. He felt weak and sick. Singapore? Fleeting shadows of doubt kept prancing across his mind. He fought them. No! He wouldn't permit them to soften him, weaken him. Damn it, no! The fall of Singapore couldn't under any circumstances be considered even a faint possibility ... No! He kept saying it to himself. But in unguarded moments the faint possibility took form in his mind and he was appalled and horrified because if that faint possibility turned out to be true, then the whole thing would have been a farce, an utterly pointless exercise in killing and being killed.... And he kept thinking of Louise laughing like hell.

'Hullo, old boy.'

It was Mike Gibbs. Unshaven but wearing a large smile.

'Hullo, Mike. My back hurts.'

'I imagine it does. I just took a bullet out of it.'

'It wasn't a bullet. It was a turd.'

'What?'

'Never mind, sorry.'

'How on earth did you manage to get a bullet there? It's almost exactly the same spot Kerr got shot in.'

'Odd coincidence, eh?'

'Yes, rather.' Mike wiped his neck with a grubby handkerchief. 'Well, you can take it easy now, old man. Rest. Get your strength back.'

'What time is it?'

'Don't worry about the time.'

'I must.' But it was difficult to remember why. Gibbs walked away. With an effort Cornish recalled his own watch. He dragged his arm up.

Nearly twelve.

Weakly Cornish lay back and wondered about being alive and having failed. A man snored chokingly nearby; another talked in a low monotone. The smell was foul.

All I've done, Cornish thought, is to make a bad situation infinitely worse. Why didn't Kerr shoot me dead? It would have been kinder. Perhaps that was why he didn't do it.

He drifted into a semi-comatose state in which a man with red veins in his nose measured him for a suit and then ripped buttons and badges from it.

The crack of artillery woke him. The earth shuddered. Above him, the bamboo roof trembled as if in fear.

'They're off again,' said one man.

'Rotten bastards,' said another.

Cornish closed his eyes. He heard the men moving; he pictured them huddling, burying their heads, instinctively trying to protect themselves.

The shells burst on the north side of the hill with deep, slightly muffled sounds. Occasionally a round would hit the crest or land on the south face; then the din was terrifying: an angry, blatant blast followed by a shower of dirt and bracken, stones and earth.

Cornish wished for a direct hit. An end to it all. Fast, merciful, efficient. There was nothing left to hope for. His life had already ended as surely as if Kerr had placed the bullet between his eyes.

He lay there listening to the thunder of the shelling, feeling the fragments of God-knows-what falling on his face. Minutes passed. Each deepened his misery. Then, quite suddenly, he was fired with the desire to get back to the north face, to die there, facing the enemy instead of lying like some helpless vegetable. The manner of his dying had become a matter of all-consuming importance.

He didn't pause to consider the matter. He pushed himself sideways with his right arm. All the fires of hell streaked up his back. He bit his lips and felt the tears filling his eyes as he started to crawl.

'David, for God's sake—'

Mike Gibbs clutched at his shoulder.

'Let go, Mike, please.'

'Where the hell do you think you're going?'

'Up there ... I've got to.'

'Don't be a fool. You can't.

'I can, Mike.'

'You're wounded, for God's sake.'

'I don't care. I've got to go. Please help me.'

'Help you? Are you mad?'

'It's the only way. Give me a stick or something.'

'No.'

'Please, Mike.'

* * *

The shells rained down. Explosion merged with explosion to form a continuous, lunatic din. Dirt and smoke tumbled in the air; the earth shivered.

The British troops clutched their ears as they clung to the mud and filth of their dug-outs. Some were snatched bodily to spin helplessly above the hill, their arms and legs fluttering like inadequate wings. Some men survived near misses only to be buried in soil that crushed the breath and life out of them before they had time to be frightened. Still others vanished in the incredible fury of direct hits: one instant they were breathing, reasoning human beings, the next instant they were umpteen miniscule particles darting through the air like sticky insects that fell at last with barely enough weight in them to bend a blade of grass.

But still more men survived although their nerves were shredded and their heads pounded as though they had been beaten by clenched fists. Most men clung to the earth and thought only of survival; others forced themselves to get to their feet between blasts and snatch glances at the enemy, to see whether he was on the move again. Not yet. Thank Christ. Head down again, buried between shoulder blades.

Cornish kept telling himself: I've got to remain conscious. It's important, very important. But he kept forgetting why; again and again he had to think it out. Had to get up the hill. Had to get to the top. To fight.

The stick slipped from his hand and slithered away down the slope, bouncing and bounding as if pleased to get away from him.

No matter; it was no damn good; it was a stupid burden.... A man could crawl without a stick.

Why did he have to get to the top?

To fight. Yes, to fight.

He reached out, clutched a handful of grass and pulled

himself a few inches. Now the other hand: a few more inches. He felt the earth shuddering beneath him as it absorbed the awful impact of the shells. Tiny particles of dirt spattered down on him. Some fell in his half-open mouth. It tasted bitter. He dragged himself a few more inches, gasping out obscenities; but gasping out obscenities was too exhausting.

Mustn't pass out. Terribly important not to pass out.

Had the shelling spared a single soul? Surely by now every square inch of the hill had been hit again and again. He looked back. He seemed to have been crawling for hours yet he was only a little more than half-way up the hill.

He ducked as five shells exploded two hundred yards ahead of him and above him. A neat row of eruptions, equally spaced, springing to equal heights. A tree toppled sideways. But for some reason it stopped falling at an angle of forty-five degrees; its branches and leaves hung like limp hair.

Now there was a new noise. For an instant Cornish thought Kerr's prophecy had come true. Across the hill in loose formation flew half a dozen aircraft. They were twin-engined jobs, but not transports. They didn't carry ammo and supplies for the hard-pressed defenders of the hill—only bombs to blow them to pieces.

The airmen wasted no time. Bombs tumbled out of their machines' bellies to curve down through the muggy air and explode with piercing cracks all along the lines of trenches on the north face.

Huddled on the slope, Cornish could hear the bombs and could see the debris spinning through the air. Again and again, the bombers roared directly over him, turning after their bomb runs. He crawled against a clump of bushes but he felt horribly exposed. How could they fail to see him? Their faces, framed in leather flying gear, turned to him behind glinting canopies. Perhaps they thought him dead. ... The bombers' engines snarled and the air quivered, elbowed this way and that by the bursting bombs.

In horrified fascination, Cornish watched a string of bombs burst in a line starting at the top of the hill and aiming directly for him. One, two, three, four, five ... the next one would hit him fair and square. But there wasn't a sixth bomb. The bomber sped away to the south then banked sharply. The explosions stank, an acid poisonous stink. For an instant he wondered if it was gas. Gas was, after all, a very logical solution to the problem of the hill and its doughty defenders.

Oh Christ, get it over with, he thought. He was going to die; he was sure of it; who could survive this holocaust?

He was wryly interested to observe that as the last vestiges of hope vanished, so did all his fear. There was nothing left to be afraid of.

A bomber came streaking over the brow of the hill. Its nose machine-gun blazed. Zap, zap, zap: the bullets tore into the ground, sending earth and dirt spraying ahead. Cornish saw a man in the conical transparent nose of the bomber staring bleakly down at him, swinging his machine-gun, attempting to compensate for the speed of the aircraft. The bullets swept past Cornish, each round double-cracking as the air suddenly filled the vacuum caused by its passing.

Missed, you bastard, he breathed; weakly he raised his hand and made a V-sign at the bomber. It turned abruptly, its broad wing pointing down at the dressing station. For a lunatic moment, Cornish imagined the pilot angrily turning his aircraft because of the rude gesture. Tiny dots of light flickered at the rear gunner's position.

'You missed too, you sod ...'

He turned back to the task of dragging himself up the hill. It looked enormous, a vast unbeatable slope. He thrust one hand forward, dug his fingers into the dirt, strained to heave himself forward.

It was then that the Jap planes attacked the dressing-station.

Even as he saw them dropping bombs on the crazy patchwork of bamboo and canvas, he said aloud, 'God, they don't realize it's a hospital!' That had to be the reason because there was no point in it, nothing whatsoever to be gained by it.

The first bomb hit the ledge fifty yards from the wounded men. The second landed on the path. The third landed squarely in the centre of the target sending up a shaft of flame and smoke and broken bodies. A sheet fluttered in pathetic flight. A naked man turned slowly in the air and then fell, to bounce like some discarded toy. More bombs fell, murderously, mercilessly accurate.

The bombers turned over their victims, their wings dull grey and green, with the solid red symbol of the Rising Sun on the tips.

'No,' Cornish yelled, still somehow convinced that the airmen were making an honest error. 'It's the dressing-station, you idiots!'

But more bombs fell. More shuddering blasts ripped through tents and *atap* shelters. The whole flimsy mess was flying to pieces and blazing as if eager for its own destruction. Men, wounded, feeble, could be seen trying to find cover where there was no cover. One man tried to follow Cornish up the slope but the machine-guns got him and he lay in a swamp of his own blood.

Now the bombers methodically machine-gunned the remains. It was easy. Everything lay in a straight line along the ledge. All the pilots had to do was follow it. The gunners did the rest.

Cornish buried his head in his hands. He couldn't look.

It was mad, purposeless. A ghastly, unspeakable mistake. And he was responsible. He could have prevented it. A voice kept stating the fact. He wanted to stop the voice and say that he had done his best, but he had no control over the voice.

The earth heaved beneath him as if shaken by some giant's hand deep inside. Dirt rained on him. A pebble stung his hand.

Then, abruptly, the din ceased.

21

Company after company of Japanese infantry trudged from the shelter of the jungle. As they took the open slope, they bent their bodies forward, their rifles swinging easily before them. From beneath steel helmet-rims their dark eyes peered up at the British positions. The hateful, stubborn British! This time they had to be defeated. It was a categorical order. There could be no failures tolerated. Threats of mass courts-martial, even summary executions, had underlined the orders. The hill must be taken. At any cost.

Kerr placed his feet precisely eighteen inches apart on the soggy ground outside the cave. He eased his back against the wall of earth. God, what a relief; it took some of the weight from his body. He could stand up like a man at least, even if he was leaning back a bit. He could hold his Webley and converse with the men milling around him, preparing for the Japs. Good lads, every one of them ... they had taken everything the Japs had to offer—and, hell, it was enough—and they hadn't broken. Their spirit was too strong. A soldier's spirit meant everything; he might be physically exhausted but his spirit could keep him going until he won.

Who had told him that? And when?

Milne, face a-stream with sweat, stood panting before him. So many men killed, approximately; so many men wounded, approximately ... and some sort of shambles in Sick Quarters ... but no time to discuss it ... hordes of Jap infantry on the way ... the men still managing to give him a grin and a thumbs-up....

Damn good lads, Kerr thought. He looked up at the sky. God, the bloody air force *had* to get through. And soon.

Cornish found himself hating the hill as he might hate another person. The pain kept swarming over him in waves of increasing savagery. Consciousness kept slipping; the hill became an enormous man, obese and ugly, who mocked his feeble efforts at progress, who pushed him back as if he were a kitten, who threatened to stamp on him and squash him into the dirt. His body kept stretching, the bones pulling from their sockets, the nerves and muscles straining, quivering, about to snap.

Then the rifle-fire began. A rattle. A dry rattle.

Oh Christ, he thought. Now he heard the deeper thump-thump of the Brens. Men were shouting.

Nearly there ... God, nearly there.

His fingers, raw and bleeding, dug deeply into the earth as he pulled himself the last few feet. The half-fallen tree stood over him. He crawled into its shadow. He was at the top! Now he was on level ground. He could take his weight on his elbows and pull himself along—like a jungle-crawling creature, he thought, and saw colour-plates from the encyclopedia and David Edward Cornish among the lizards and snakes.

The tinny, lightweight sound of the Japanese machine-guns was continuous. Endless streams of scalding bullets pouring into the British positions. The air was foul with the stink of explosive. Dimly he thought about Guy Fawkes night and being achingly tired because of running for miles and Ferris being only yards behind and still half a mile to go and boys waving caps and cheering the leaders on to victory and the greater glory of Cornwallis House ... and how fitting, David, to see you end up like this ... you always lacked *something*.... Suddenly, weirdly, he wondered what his parents would think to see him now. And the relations, the parchment-faced aunts, the uncles, cousins, etcetera. What about all of the relatives who had died? Were they watching him? Cheering him on? Having a bloody good laugh?

He stopped. He lay, panting. He even slept for a few fevered moments. He had to think where he was.

Then he was aware of a change in the noises coming from below. The tone had changed. The pitch. There were more voices. More yells.

He had to hurry! Move! Come on, man! Painfully, he dragged himself the last few yards. He reached forward and clutched the point where the ground began to slope to the north.

He had an appallingly good view of the battle's final moments.

He watched as the first Japanese died clutching for the rifles of the British soldiers. More Japanese swarmed over their comrades' bodies. Some fell. Others broke through the defenders' line, shooting, stabbing with their bayonets. A Tommy hurled two Japs back on to the hill using his rifle as a staff. A third Jap shot him. Milne killed one with his revolver. An instant later he folded up as a Japanese bayonet was buried to its hilt in his back.

It was a squirming, struggling mass of humanity, all reason lost as every ounce of energy became dedicated to slaughter. They fired until their magazines were empty, then they slashed and stabbed and killed or were killed.

The rest of the line was holding. But it didn't mean anything now. It was too late; a breach had been punched; the enemy was pouring through. Desperately, the British troops tried to hold them. Men died in grotesque heaps; the ground became slippery with blood; men skidded and fell in it and their uniforms were bright with the stuff.

Every step back admitted another score of the stocky men with the tall rifles and glittering bayonets. Men flopped in the ugly relaxation of death. They vanished under advancing boots.

Cornish saw Firmin's body slither loosely into a trench, head first, like some bit of poultry slung on to the counter.

Now the Japanese swelled in both directions along the road. They were behind the trenches. They yelled and gesticulated to one another. They laughed in the moment of their triumph. One Jap dropped his helmet. He stooped to pick it up; a bullet hit him in the centre of his skull.

For the first time, Cornish saw Kerr.

He was farther along the line, organizing a barricade across the road. Men were grabbing ammunition boxes and kit and sandbags, anything their frenzied fingers fell upon. They flung the stuff in the road and hurled themselves down behind it and shoved clips of ammunition into their rifles and worked their bolts and fired like madmen at the approaching Japs.

Kerr was standing among them. *Standing*. Pointing. Talking. Indicating. He stuck his pipe in his mouth.

Like a spectator at a football match, Cornish found himself urging the home team on to one final effort.... You can beat the bastards.... Yes, you can ... you know you can ... try, for God's sake, try!

It took an effort to remember, to return to reality.

Kerr stood in the centre of the road, his men on either side of him. He rested his revolver on the crook of his left arm and fired with steady precision. When the Webley was empty, he passed it back to McGregor who reloaded it. As he handed the weapon back to Kerr, McGregor folded up and fell, becoming a strangely tiny mound of tattered khaki.

It was as if, instantly, death had shrunken him. Kerr glanced down at him between shots. He emptied his revolver again, broke it open, stuffed in fresh cartridges as he bellowed to the men. When he had reloaded he held the gun above his head and gesticulated with his left arm. He was yelling, his face crimson, his white teeth sparkling ... and the men were turning to him, nodding, agreeing, some even grinning with the fierce joy of irrevocability. Kerr gesticulated, pointed, his thick fingers jabbing the air like pistons. He took a step forward, an agonizing, faltering step—and instantly the men were around him, supporting him, clustering around him as they fired at the enemy and fell.

Cornish stared in numbed, horrified fascination.

They were *charging*. The crazy, marvellous idiots were surging forward. It was pitiful, futile—suicidal. A tatty bunch of scarecrows hurrying forward to topple, a dozen at a time, limbs a-sprawl, rifles bouncing on the road as they fell from lifeless hands.

But it was as if an entirely new creature had been created; an amalgam of men and their courage and will. The creature began to die even as it was born: it diminished: it left parts of itself lying on the road, instantly forgotten, for the parts no longer contributed to the whole and there was no time for any fraction of an instant of the past: only the present mattered now: and the present consisted of covering the last remaining yards and firing the last remaining rounds and staving off the inevitable for the maximum number of instants.

Bullets made in Shimizu and Nagoya found their marks in men from Shropshire and Lincolnshire and Cheshire and Roxburgh.

But still the rest of them struggled on and still Kerr was the nucleus, still bellowing, exhorting, thrusting himself forward. Now it seemed he was driving the creature on instead of being carried by it.

He was among the last to fall.

Like a brave bull in the *corrida de toros*, he lurched and tumbled. And staggered to his feet. And fell again. He kept firing. On his hands and knees he crawled, a few agonizing inches at a time. Around him, the Japanese bullets snapped on the road and whined away into the distance. Still Kerr kept going; still he moved, in spite of them. Still he breathed; still his mouth framed mocking curses.

But at last he was silenced.

Face down he slumped to lie with arms and legs extended as if to cover with his body as much of the road as possible. His fingers clutched at the ground; his toes dug into the loose surface.

The pain dissolved, leaving only a vague glow. He felt quite grand in a dozy sort of way. And satisfied, for the whole job, the one known as duty, had at long last been done. And, he might add, done bloody well. Even Louise had to admit it. A bit grudgingly perhaps, but she did, and that was the important thing. And well might Brian look proud of his dad. Bonny little bugger. And the train was still roaring on towards Manchester and he had to move sharpishly if he was going to make this splendid creature in the powder blue aware of his existence. A moment for tie-straightening; but his boots, his laboriously polished boots, were spattered with mud and blood ... Somehow the bullets kept sizzling past him, hundreds, thousands of them —how could they possibly keep on missing? One of the pleasantest things was knowing that there would never again be a need for anger and frustration over thwarted ambition. The high-born gents were absolutely, irrevocably robbed of their power to hurt.

He was glad he had never gone back to the pub near Hertford.

When a Japanese soldier turned the body over with his boot, he found Kerr smiling. Thinking the Englishman still alive, the soldier shot him in the forehead. But the smile remained on Kerr's lips.

Now only a scattering of men still fired at the Japanese. And within a few moments they were running, trying desperately to escape. But it was hopeless. There was nowhere for them to go. Relaxed now because it was no longer a battle, the Japanese troops took leisurely aim and killed the Tommies as they ran.

Cornish squeezed his eyes shut and flattened his hands against his ears but still he heard laughs, nervous little shrieky laughs as the victors had their sport.

The minutes passed. There were single shots, loud and frightening, and fusillades, ragged and furious. Cornish imagined a score of Japs firing at one fleeing Tommy, riddling him.

He crawled into a broad-leaved bush and pulled the foliage behind him. He could just see part of the slope; he caught glimpses of Japanese soldiers examining dead Tommies, chuckling over their belongings. When they found a man still alive they put paid to him with a bullet or bayonet. The shots were like the crack of the trainer's whip at Bertram Mills'.

He waited. Soon they would find him. He wished fervently that he might have died with his comrades, in battle. But he had forfeited the right; he had proved himself unworthy. Wearily, hopelessly, he shook his head. The words sounded so sickeningly melodramatic—yet, God, they were true!

He heard footsteps.

He tried to disappear into the thorny embrace of the bush. The Japs were coming nearer but he still couldn't see them.

Their boots were thudding like dull drum-beats. And their damned hateful voices were clearly audible now. Then, through the leaves, he saw them. They ambled along, their Model-99 rifles at the ready. Their flat-cheeked faces moved from side to side, their eyes darting about as if following the path of an erratic fly.

Cornish clung to the earth, hardly daring to breathe. He caught glimpses of the soldiers' grey and green caps and their grubby puttees. One of the Japs stopped to urinate only yards away. A few drops spattered through the tall grass to fall on Cornish's hand. He closed his eyes, squeezed them tightly as the terror and the pain and the shame beat at him. God, did even *he* deserve to die this way, clutching the earth like some mindless animal? And hadn't he sincerely believed his actions right and proper? If so, why did his very being shrivel with shame?

The Japs moved away, their voices fading. He lay perfectly still. He could *feel* a Jap standing behind him, watching him and waiting for him to move.

He held his breath until his lungs seemed about to rupture.

He turned, quickly, fearfully, wincing with the pain and the anticipated sight. But there was no Jap.

He felt weak and sick. He lay still, not knowing what to do next. The foliage seemed thicker a few yards to the left. He decided to hide in it. It seemed the only sensible course of action open to him. He clutched at a tree and pulled himself on to his hands and knees. He held his breath, feeling his consciousness wobbling. I mustn't pass out, he thought; if I do, they'll find me.

They'll find you anyway. Eventually.

Nevertheless, I've got to try. I've viewed the situation with as much objectivity as I can muster and I'm taking the course of action ...

He moved out of the thicket.

The Japanese soldier was looking straight at him.

A thick-set fellow wearing a soft cap, he stood twenty yards away, smoking a cigarette in the observant way of all soldiers who snatch illegal smokes.

That buggers it, thought Cornish, past emotion.

The Japanese soldier's rifle was leaning against a tree. It rattled in a curiously loose fashion as he took it and slung it from right hand to left, his eyes fixed on Cornish.

I'm wounded and unarmed, Cornish thought but didn't say.

The Japanese blew the cigarette from his lips as he tugged back on his rifle bolt. He walked towards Cornish, his right hand encircling the stock, his finger entering the trigger guard.

'Get it over with,' said Cornish.

'*Nani?*'

'I'm not going to beg, you sod.'

The soldier stopped five yards away and took aim.

'Please don't shoot him!'

Cornish turned. So did the Japanese.

Tom Byrne stood there, holding a service Webley at arm's length, both hands around the grip. The weapon wobbled ludicrously; it seemed far too heavy for the priest, threatening to tip him over.

The Japanese soldier's rifle still pointed at Cornish but his eyes flashed uncertainly between Tom and back.

Oh good God, thought Cornish, numbed, whatever next?

Tom said, 'Don't kill him. I beg you. Just go away.'

Cornish said, 'Talk in Japanese, Tom. You said you could.'

Tom said, 'Yes, but I must think ... I...'

It happened in an instant; it was over almost as rapidly. The Jap suddenly swung his rifle towards Tom Byrne and fired. The bullet caught the priest just below the heart. The Webley discharged.

A bird shrieked in terror as the Japanese soldier toppled sideways, his left eye a bright red pulp. His body thudded loosely into the tall grass and was almost hidden.

Cornish scrambled to where Tom lay. Blood was spreading, staining the coarse robes. There was no dignity. One bare leg thrust out of the muddle of cloth: a skinny, unlovely leg. Tom's eyes were open but his face was colourless.

'Tom—'

'Did I kill that man, David? I didn't mean to shoot at all ... the gun went off. ... Did I kill him?'

Cornish looked at the Jap. He was a grim sight: exudation mingled with blood around his mouth and nostrils.

'He looks dead.' Cornish tried to smile. 'Thanks very much.'

'I just ... just wanted him to go away.'

'He did, Tom, in a way.'

The priest's face twisted in pain. 'I'm going to die, David. Yes, I am quite sure of it. You know, in moments of sinful pride I imagined a bishop or even a cardinal present to officiate during my last moments on earth.' A grin, weak, fragile. 'Instead I have my atheistic friend, David Cornish. There's a gentle irony in there, don't you think?'

'I'll get Mike Gibbs.'

'No, it's quite pointless, David, believe me. I am dying. I am content. Don't be unhappy for me. I want to ask you something, though: please find the pyx. It is in the black purse I wear...'

Cornish had to fumble through the blood-sticky robes. At last he found it. With trembling fingers he opened it; inside it was lined with white silk; it contained a silver case about the size of a pocket watch.

'Good, thank you, David. Open it, please. I can't.'

Tom's voice was no more than a whisper. Cornish had to strain to hear him. He fumbled with the pyx, conscious of probing into secrets to which he had no right. The case sprang open. In the scratched gold interior lay two thin wafers impressed with the sign of the Cross.

'My prayer-book, David. It is in my robe.'

Cornish found it, its page edges crusted with blood.

'I have it, Tom.'

'Will you read a prayer?'

'Of course.'

'Find ... the Prayers for the Dying.'

'Tom.'

'Please, David. And place the host on my tongue.'

'The ... host?'

'From the pyx...'

Cornish did as the priest asked. The tiny wafer was flimsy and insubstantial but as it touched the priest's tongue his lips curved into the ghost of a smile.

Cornish read: 'Go forth from this world, O Christian soul, in the name of God the Father Almighty, who created you...'

Cornish had to blink the tears away. Through a blur he found the next line and began to read. He stopped. Tom Byrne couldn't hear any more. His eyes were open but they were misty, lifeless. He looked peaceful. Cornish touched the priest's face. It was still warm; the sweat hadn't had time to dry.

He picked up the Webley and opened it. All six rounds had been fired. Tom must have used the last one.

'You're a lucky sod, Cornish.'

With difficulty he straightened Tom Byrne's limbs and placed the prayer book in his hands, closing the thin fingers over the cover. He pulled a corner of the robe over the priest's face.

He listened. Just the noise of animals. And the dry panting of the two legged creature that was him.

He had no recollection of falling asleep. His eyes must simply have closed in utter exhaustion. He slept a troubled sleep dreaming of endless streets and howling winds and sweating faces smeared with blood and snot and triggers that turned soft and useless when you needed them.

When he awoke, the sun was low.

And Watanabe was looking down at him, two soldiers beside him, with bayonets clipped to the muzzles of their rifles.

'We meet again, Captain,' said Watanabe.

Cornish nodded automatically, thinking of Vera Lynn singing a song with a title rather like that. Oh Christ, now it really was all up, that sod Watanabe finding him.... Still, it had to happen eventually.... Dully his mind tried to cope with all that had happened.

'Are you seriously wounded?'

'Not seriously. But painfully.'

Watanabe said formally, 'You are my prisoner, Captain.'

What's left of me, Cornish thought. He was shaky with fatigue. Somehow he didn't know quite what to feel. Regret and relief nestled together like adulterers. It was all unquestionably over. No more need to hide. Or hope.

'Are you able to get up?'

'Yes, I think so.'

Watanabe rapped out an order in Japanese. One of the soldiers grasped Cornish's shoulder and hoisted him to his feet. The action was too violent. Pain slashed through Cornish's body. A croak of agony escaped his lips; he almost fell.

Angered, Watanabe snapped at the man, who hung his head like a chastised infant.

'They are pigs some of them,' said Watanabe. 'Ignorant

211

peasants. Are you all right?'

'I'll live,' said Cornish. Then wondered.

'One of our medical officers will examine your wound,' said Watanabe. 'I shall see to it. Then you will be transferred to Singapore. A prisoner of war camp is being organized there.'

'Are the others going there too?' Cornish asked.

Watanabe didn't answer for a moment. He frowned and looked away and shrugged like a man disowning responsibility for the actions of other men. Then he said:

'I must tell you that I know of no others, Captain. You appear to be the privileged one.'

22

Now I stand on the slope above the road. I look down on the untidy, pot-holed surface and I can almost see the bodies stretched out, limbs loosely, awkwardly splayed.

That road is hallowed ground to me.

I walk along the crest of the hill, and I watch the jungle moving, living. There is no clue that a battle was ever fought here. What did I expect? A memorial? A plaque? It was a minor skirmish, I tell myself, in a war that nobody wishes to remember.

The *kampong* is rebuilt. The citizens glance at me and speak to one another about me. No doubt they ask what this European is doing, walking and looking about him as if searching for something. Perhaps the older folk feel uneasy—as well they might: for Europeans have always meant trouble.

The trees, the foliage, the multi-coloured flowers: they all flourish, as if high explosive had never torn through them. The slope, too, looks so bloody innocent.

Have I, in my stupidity, come to the wrong hill?

No. I look around. This, as they say, is the place. And it has recovered, in spite of us. The wounds have healed.

I stroll to where Tom Byrne died. He killed a man for me—and it troubled him in his last agonized moments. Are you watching me, Tom? I wonder. I often think of you. I often see people who remind me of you. Once, when I was in America, on business, I went to Lackawanna. But no one I spoke to remembered you or your family. I'm sorry, I say, as if it still might matter to him.

I make my way down the hill, treading with care on the steep incline. The grass is slippery; it seems to be sweating as hard as I am. I jog the last few paces to the road. There, the stones stab into the thin soles of my civilian shoes. My back stings—because of the gluteal muscles, so my doctor says. They mended somewhat less than perfectly in the gaol at Changi.

I wonder about Captain Watanabe. Did he survive the war? I hope so. Perhaps today he makes motorbikes. Or runs an advertising agency.

I walk slowly along the road, pausing as I try to identify where Kerr was finally stilled. At last I find it. Yes, this has to be the spot. I can almost see where his fingers and toes dug into the ground.

I bid Ernie a final farewell. I still respect his memory. A 'grand' soldier indeed, was Ernie Kerr and I'm sorry that I failed him. But I did what I thought was The Right Thing.

Yet I must admit I didn't want to die for that place. Dying mattered to me, but not to him. Perhaps I should be ashamed of caring so much about not dying. But I'm not ashamed. Not now.

The wind is stronger. The jungle stirs. I remember some of our men escaping into that jungle when the Japanese overran the line. To my knowledge none was ever seen again.

Mr Appleby is waiting, standing and looking at a village girl, his jaw working ruminatively.

I tell him we can go back.

'Already?' He seems surprised.

I explain that I have done what I came to do. Though God only knows what it was.

We return to where our driver is waiting. As I step into the car I look back. Yes, there *is* a memento: a tree that

214

leans at forty-five degrees. Incredibly, it is still alive.
 'All set, boss?'
 'All set,' I tell the driver, and we move off in a cloud of dust.